# Praise for: *how to Make Yourself and Influen*

"The Svengali System" in *how to Make Friends with Yourself and Influence People* takes you into deep hypnotic rapport and then shows you how to do the same thing. Excellent insights into applied influence. I enjoyed it cover to cover and was impressed with the multitude of examples and specific applications. Put this book in your library, now.

**Kevin Hogan, Author of The Science of Influence.**

# How to make Friends with Yourself and Influence People

## JONATHAN CHASE

Published by the Academy of Hypnotic Arts ltd.
www.jonathanchase.com

published by
The Academy of Hypnotic Arts Ltd.
PO Box 82 . Dawlish . Devon . EX7 0JE
www.svengalisystem.com

© *Jonathan Chase 2009*

First printed edition 2010
ISBN Number: 978-0-9547098-9-1

# Contents

# Acknowledgements

I'd like to thank a few people who have made this book possible. Although I speak a good book I tend to ramble and go off at tangents and don't type very quickly so to get this to you took a team to which I'd like to say thanks.

**Special Thanks to:**
Eric Carr for taking the original installation course, giving me feedback and asking damn awkward questions and finally for transcribing and ghost writing my verbal muttering into this book, for that alone he needs a medal.

Marisa Cohen who was responsible for compiling the action sections.

Jane Bregazzi for her editing of the bits I wrote directly, formatting, motivation and support.

Jeff Stephens, Reg Blackwood, Sharon Stiles, John B, Wayne Trice and the others who were ready and willing to take their lives to another dimension. Without these people this book wouldn't have got as far as it has.

We all need people to interact with and that's what this book is about - learning about ourselves and ultimately how to get to the people who will readily interact with us. So if you and I have interacted at all, anytime, past, present or future, I thank you as well.

Smiles :-) JonC

# About The Author

Hypnotist Edutainer Jonathan Chase hails from an English Midlands coal mining background.

Born in '55 with the debilitating neuromuscular condition Charcot Marie Tooth Syndrome.

A former Roadie, Nurse and Stage Hypnotist he has used his progressive disability as a spur to develop the skills of Influence and Persuasion. Initially as a survival method but then as a reputation building way to inspire and steer those around him to achieve an enhanced lifestyle and to gain more respect and time by inspiring and influencing those around them.

He is a leading author of hypnosis books:

Deeper and Deeper - the secrets of stage hypnosis

Don't look in his eyes - How to be a confident original hypnotist

Several Hypnotic Handbooks:

Are you Hypnotised?

Hypnotically Speaking - be a mesmeric public speaker

Seductive Suggestion - how to talk yourself into anything

and hundreds of Articles and Blog posts.

He lives in Devon near the English Riviera with his partner in life and business Jane Bregazzi although he travels extensively conducting live learning experiences and speaking.

# How to use this "Installation" book

This book has no chapters and no chapter titles. This isn't laziness, it was designed to happen like that.

I stopped teaching in favour of installing stuff in my students heads and minds because I figure if something is worth knowing and writing about then it's worth using.

This book is based on the live calls I conducted on the first Svengali System live telephone learning experience. It's formatted the way it is to recreate that experience as best we can in print.

Obviously that will never be as impacting as the original live spoken word but it can be effective and come bloody close if you put aside your criticising brain and let your subconscious mind play and ride the coaster.

Read each 'Installation' as if you were listening to the call. To install the information I am using the methods which have served hypnotists and other influencers for centuries and the ones I am presenting to you here.

If you are of the opinion that conversational 'covert' influence and suggestion only started with one guy in the 1920's or another in the 70's, think again.

Compounding, pattern interrupts, presupposition and all the other 'in-speak' are modern labels of ancient arts. They have been around as long as speech and just because they became observed, intellectualised and written about in the last century doesn't mean they have been improved.

Discovering a complex way of explaining something only appears to make it better. It's perceived value. And of course that also makes it more profitable which is the real reason for being taught more than you need to know. Someone somewhere profits from it.

Personally I prefer to profit from simplification, so what you won't find in this book is loads of bullshit for the sake of it.

Although I can't guarantee this in the way I can with a real live event, this book is as much an installation as the live call teleseminars it's based on. My Intent is to give you the basis of everything and to do that by embedding it into your subconscious using the method itself.

Don't read this as bedtime reading or in snippets on the way to work, it won't work that way. Set some time aside. Do not multitask and read each Installation in full. Then do the action described in the action summary.

If you don't then again you will not be getting the very best from the format of this book.

To strengthen the book  I suggest you repeat read each section at least twice. Repetition works much better than doing something once.

Finally, do it. The things I tell you to do you Must do. Without the advantage of being with you to hold you accountable I'm trusting you to actually do this stuff. Because once you do your life will change and so will the lives of everyone you connect with.

Don't do it and all you  have in your hands is a waste of space.

At the end of the book I'll tell you  how you can contact me to tell me how great you've done.

*Jon Chase*

# CLASS 1

Intent and Rapport - The Subconscious 9 year old
Perfect Place and the Container
Core Rapport - The Secret of True Intent
Disregarding The Unpredictable

# Core Rapport

Not so long ago I did a thing, and it isn't mine, but it shocked me so much, and it gave me so much, that even though it was only months ago, the process of going through this thing that I am going to teach you now has changed my intent unbelievably. It changed it even though I have spent years and years and years coming really from disability where you have to get really good at getting people to help you (because if you don't life gets bloody hard, which is where most of my skill comes from). We all have these talents you know.

The first step of this, I'm going to call Core Rapport, and it's step one of Intent.

Rapport means friendship to most people, doesn't it? But that's not actually what it is. It's got nothing to do with liking somebody or trusting somebody.

Being in rapport and having rapport is about having the same desires and having the same goal. That's what rapport is.

What you want to do is get into the position where the person you are talking with has exactly the same desires and goals as you. How we create that is what you'll learn in this book.

I've got to tell you why we're leaving such big gaps between the lessons. It's to allow your subconscious mind to cogitate all of this, to think about it, to create the new reality that you're going to have at the end of it.

I'm not so much teaching you this, **I'm INSTALLING** it – although some of this stuff you do have to do – but I'm elated to start, so I won't give you anything hard to do, or anything to do that I wouldn't do myself or have time to do.

But in the **Core Rapport** section, which is the next section, you are going to have to give yourself a present. And that present is two or three hours. It took me four hours to do this, but it's entirely up to you how much time you spend.

Over the next 24 hours you'll say, "Oh, I can't possibly find four hours." YES YOU CAN! It's one and a half movies. It's a long lunch. It's the time that you could get up a couple hours early and go to bed a couple of hours late.

If you're not worth four hours, you might as well put this book down, and just jack it all in and go off and get a job and work for somebody else.

Playing with these things is going to require you to do this initial setup, because what you're going to do now with Core Rapport is going to make your intent so easy, so clear, so lacking in doubt, that when you go into a situation and you really know what it is you want to do, then the people around you are going to be magically and magnetically drawn to do that.

And it's not going to require you to know loads of language patterns. You haven't got to make up clever metaphors. If you can – great! Fantastic! But that's not the point of it. You haven't got to do these things.

**Being in rapport with others is hard work unless you are in rapport with yourself.** That's why I'm calling this Core Rapport. I know it's going to sound strange and weird to those of you who aren't hypnotists. Some of you may have already come across this before. If you have, then great – you should have already done it. If you haven't, now is the time.

You must do it because the rest of what I'm going to teach and install in this book just simply will not work if you don't put the effort in at this point. I need to be able to install this into your core self, and if you don't know who your core self is, then all the barriers are going to be up, the mask is going to be in place. And by "mask" I mean, "Oh I'm a hypnotist," or "Oh, I'm a marketer," or "Oh, I'm a financial adviser," or "Oh I'm a film editor" or whatever it is you do.

Again, *being in rapport with others is hard work unless you are in rapport with yourself.*

I can't even describe what this thing has done for me. I really can't. "Awesome" is a word that doesn't even get close. I have for many, many years been playing a role as we all do, but that role fitted what everybody wanted me to be, and the more dissipated I had become, the more I tried to fit everybody's role (you know: husband, father, hypnotist, trainer, speaker, author, and all the roles that we've got – complete and utter shit that I thought was important), the more I got into all that, the thinner I got. And the further away I got from who I really was.

Now since doing this, I've got back in touch with who I am, and that to me has been so awesome, the first thing I wanted to do was teach it. In fact, this has probably been the turning point of me actually coming up with this system, because I didn't want to write it before.

And that's why I've called it the Svengali System, because that's the real me talking. We've called it the Svengali System because it's funny, it's out there and it's maverick and so am I!

This is the ultimate "boy's toy." This is the way you can play the game of life, and not take it so seriously, because taking it seriously is going to hold you back and take you down to where you are.

You know, it would be dead easy for me to say, "The first thing I'm going to teach you is about language patterns, the second thing I'm going to teach you is about trance states, the third thing I'm going to teach you about is metaphors, the fourth thing I'm going to teach you about is blah blah blah blah blah." But if you're not right, if you're not in Core Rapport with yourself, I'll tell you what – it won't work. Or it will work haphazardly. Or it will work in little bits, because every interaction that you have, whether it's relationships, whether it's business, or whether it's for fun, just pure fun – you will not *get* what you want out of it if you don't *know* what you want out of it.

And I'm not saying, "Okay, I want a free lunch." Great. That's fabulous. But what does that give you? The NLP thing would say, "Always ask yourself, what is the true reward of this and what would it give you?" Well, it might make you feel good, fulfilled, satisfied, and we tend to use those kinds of phrases because we don't understand our core self.

For me, it would fill my ego up with a "Yeah, I can do that!" And that's great, that's fabulous, and I am not ashamed of that anymore in any way whatsoever. In fact, that's the whole point of the process: for my Core Rapport to feel good about what I am doing. Because once you get your Core Rapport right, I'll tell you what's going to happen.

When you get your Core Rapport right, when you know who you are, and I'm going to give you this exercise, and it might only take you an hour, but it takes most people between two and three hours – it took me four hours because I write very slowly, and I'm going to tell you that you've got to do this by hand – you must not use a computer and I'll tell you why. Doing the Core Rapport has put me back on the track to realize that some of the things I said I *should* be feeling at the end of doing something, weren't coherent with who I am. And what this will do is get you coherent with who you are.

So, how do you do it? One thing I get thrown at me a lot – and I do mean thrown at me because some people really have trouble with simplicity. They say, "This is too fuckin' easy – it can't work. This is too simple, and it just can't be done."

But I have found in my life, the one thing about being disabled is, being a disabled person teaches you that complexity is bloody hard work. And being in rapport with others is hard work unless you're in rapport with yourself.

And the last thing we want to do is work hard. We want to work smart – if it's work at all. And it shouldn't be…it should be fun! Everything that I do has to fit now three criteria, and I've laid this down:

Number one, it has to be **Easy**, because it's got to appeal to and be usable by a bright nine-year-old child. And that's what your subconscious mind is. I'll tell you about that in a second.

Number two, it has to be **Fun**. It has to be enjoyable! I want my head as much as possible to be full of dopamine because that's the feel-good drug. Not only is that the feel-good drug, but it's a proven scientific fact that when you have dopamine in place, you learn faster. You think faster. You retain more information. Those three things alone, in a social situation or a business situation are vital. They are absolutely vital to be able to think faster than everybody else, to be able to remember everything easier, and to be in that situation where you're actually enjoying the process. Think about that. And think how just filling your head full of dopamine when you go into a social situation is going to be a mega thing!

Number three it has to be **Effective**, it has to work. Now I have an unusual way of finding out what works. I do it and watch and test the result. I then give it to someone else and get them to test it in real life situations. Lots of stuff out there is class based. That is it works in a room full of people with a vested interest in making it work. Or it's personality tested. That is it's tested just by the teacher or innovator and lets face it personalities are different and some people do stuff better and more easily than others. Or worse it hasn't been tested at all and just seems like a good idea. For that reason there will be stuff you're expecting me to give you and you won't get it here because either it doesn't work or it doesn't work well enough.

Now, getting into rapport and empathy with yourself requires you to get in touch with your subconscious mind – with a bright nine-year-old child. I really do believe this, and I know I've said it in other courses and books, but I'm going to go over it in this book because it's really important and it's vital that everybody under-stands this. As you are growing up, your emotional states, your unconscious decisions – and believe me that the subconscious mind does make decisions – you act like a child.

There are a lot of people who say the subconscious doesn't make decisions, but it does. It chooses. It may choose to do something or not do something, but it makes choices. It doesn't make decisions based on experience. It doesn't make decisions based on logic. Or reason. It just makes decisions like any bright nine-year-old child.

As you go through life, up until about the age of nine if you watch children (and if you're a parent you've done that, and if not, you know, borrow somebody else's. Don't kill it…just bother it and watch it) but up until the age of nine, you act like a child, and then something starts to happen. And I'll tell you what starts to happen: logic starts to grow.

Now it could be a little bit earlier, and it could be a little bit later, and some people never get there at all. In fact, Jane says that's what happened to me!

But as the brain matures, and as the neurological pathways are formed, that logical, reasoning computer seems to take over. It's just that we use it more so it's more "out in front of us." Think of this like the subconscious mind being the user and your brain being the results of what goes through the computer and being on screen. It doesn't matter how muddled up and jumbled your mind is when you put the information into a computer, it still comes out on the screen in nice blocks and squares and plenty of words and that sort of thing.

The computer comes out with the logical stuff even though the subconscious mind is a bit addled. Now that's fine. At about the age of nine the computer gets stronger and stronger and stronger. It's as if the screen of your computer gets bigger and bigger and bigger. But behind it is still the user. And that user, because it doesn't have to anymore, because it's not in control anymore, stops maturing.

People say to me, "That's rubbish, that's complete rubbish because the subconscious mind knows how to drive a car." No it doesn't! Your *neurological system* knows how to drive a car.

Your subconscious mind knows how to notice the girl with a nice bum that's walking down the road, or why the person in front of you is weaving all over the road. The subconscious mind isn't driving the car. You're driving the car with muscle memory and very little else.

Let's separate the two. The subconscious mind is a bright nine-year-old child. Think how many times, especially when you are emotional, *especially* when you are emotional, that you are making decisions based on the same criteria as a young child uses.

"I like that. I want it. I'm going to have it!"

Immature? Yeah, sure. But after you've gone through that and after you've made those decisions, your conscious mind will logic them out and say, "Oh yes, but I needed to buy that thing or I needed to be with that person or I needed to do this and needed to do that."

I know for many, many people who are reading this, this is 101 stuff, but it isn't for everybody because not everybody's been lucky enough to find somebody who realizes that the mind and the brain – although they might be for all we know anything from separate beings altogether to the subconscious being just another process – they are two definite processes of our mental state.

One's highly emotional and creative, and the other side is solid and logical. And reasonable.

You see the bright nine-year-old child come out when we are emotional. So the one thing that you're going to be doing when I put you into the situation where I tell you what to do with the Core Rapport is you're going to pour loads of emotion into it.

To be honest, I did this myself – and I've been doing this crap for thirty years – and I thought, "Yeah, go on, I'll give it a go." And I did not expect what I got, because what I got at the end of it was I sat there with tears running down my face! It was a moving experience because I put so much emotion into it.

They were tears of, I don't know, release, joy, or maybe I'm just getting soft in my old age. Probably the latter! But – the more emotion you put into this the more value you're going to get out of it.

Most people know that when I am hypnotising I create a situation – I'm going to run through this with you right now – that I create a situation in most peoples' heads called the **Perfect Place**.

We're going to do a Perfect Place in just a moment, and I know if you've been on one of my trainings or you've been mentored by me on the phone or whatever and we've done Perfect Place then you've already got yours in there. But I still want you to go through the process because we're going to create not a different Perfect Place but we're going to create for you a different receptacle, a different container, for you to put your stuff in.

It's vital that you do this. If you haven't done this before, what I want you to do is to make sure that you're not going to be disturbed, get comfortable – you're not going to drop the book and you're not going to go into trance or hypnosis or anything like that but you are going to be focusing slightly differently.

So if you are prone to going into trance hypnosis I'm telling your subconscious mind right now that it's not necessary. Do not go in!

But what I *do* want you to do right now is in your mind's eye – and the safest way of doing this is just keep your eyes open because most people visualize with their eyes open a lot easier than they can with their eyes closed – look off into the middle distance and create a Perfect Place in your head. Describe it to yourself. And that perfect place can be anytime, anywhen – anywhere in the universe.

Inside that Perfect Place – and it really can be anywhere – nobody else can get in here because it's inside your head. When you're in that Perfect Place what I want you to do is to create a receptacle, a container of some kind. And I do want you to do something now. This is the only time I've ever controlled this, but I really need to install this in your head.

I want you to paint two letters on that receptacle or put it on the side of the receptacle or on the top or the bottom or whatever sort of receptacle it is. And those two letters are an "M" and an "E." "ME." Because that's where you're going to be putting every-thing you'll be learning in this book and on this course.

Because this is about you. Everything in this book is about you. Everything in this learning experience is about you.

Now [after you've created your Perfect Place] give yourself a shake and – brrrrrrrrrrrrrrrr – shake yourself up, okay? And just know that because that thing's in there now you don't have to worry about forgetting any of this, about accessing it consciously when you go into situations because it's just going to be there in your subconscious mind just like driving, or more importantly, just like walking. Or if you're like me, just like pushing a wheelchair or using crutches or whatever it is that you can do naturally.

It's going to be in there so don't worry about it. Okay.

Right. Step back. Have a drink of water. Okay – wide awake! Wakey Wakey.

Just in case you're a somnambulist!

\*\*\*\*\*\*\*\*\*\*\*\*\*\*\*\*\*\*\*\*\*\*\*\*\*\*\*\*\*\*\*\*\*\*\*\*\*\*\*\*\*\*\*\*\*\*\*\*\*\*\*

Note: This comes across much better on the call than it reads. The idea is to give your mind somewhere to put the stuff I'm installing so that it knows where to go to retrieve it when it needs it.

We usually just throw our experiences in there using the PIDT filing system - Put It Down There. That's the reason most memories are hard to get until we have done something often enough for our brain to know where to find it and our mind to make use of it.

Using this very simple 'container' system we are storing stuff in a place directly, so as you go through this 'see' all this stuff being written down and stored in your receptacle, your container. Then just trust it to be there when you need it.

\*\*\*\*\*\*\*\*\*\*\*\*\*\*\*\*\*\*\*\*\*\*\*\*\*\*\*\*\*\*\*\*\*\*\*\*\*\*\*\*\*\*\*\*\*\*\*\*\*\*\*\*\*\*

## Core Rapport

Why is it important to be in rapport with yourself?

Most people are spending all their time in conflict. Their conscious mind is in conflict with their subconscious mind. Because their conscious mind is trying to put the mask on, because it doesn't know who the subconscious mind is, and the subconscious mind is trying to rip the mask off because it doesn't know who the conscious mind is. And the two are constantly having a little internal battle with themselves.

Now apparently, that's the natural state of affairs. But I'll tell you what: when you've done this Core Rapport that will stop. That will end immediately.

It certainly ended with me. I am no longer in internal conflict. And I'll tell you another thing: all the bad things that have happened to me over my life have been the course of that internal conflict that I didn't even know I had. And all of the good stuff has happened in the times when it's just stopped for a little while. So this is really, really important.

You may have heard this before. I don't know who came up with this. I have a sense that it could be a Tony Robbins thing, but as

Tony Says, "you should always copy and you should always copy the best" – so if it did come from him then it probably came from somebody earlier. And it's been copied a couple of times before. But I'm not giving him credit for it because I don't know where it comes from.

\*\*\*\*\*\*\*\*\*\*\*\*\*\*\*\*\*\*\*\*\*\*\*\*\*\*\*\*\*\*\*\*\*\*\*\*\*\*\*\*\*\*\*\*\*\*\*\*\*\*

Note: I got this from Frank Kern the internet marketer, simply because he was the first I heard it from and even he admits it isn't his.

\*\*\*\*\*\*\*\*\*\*\*\*\*\*\*\*\*\*\*\*\*\*\*\*\*\*\*\*\*\*\*\*\*\*\*\*\*\*\*\*\*\*\*\*\*\*\*\*\*

But, I've tweaked it to try and make it as easy as possible for you because you're going to be taught four parts to this process.

Now the most important thing that you must do is you must not type this down on a computer, because if you're using a computer, distractions happen all the time.

I don't care how focused you are, I don't care if you think, "Oh I don't do things like that." I'm running this course here and running a learning experience here, and I have got two mobile phones, I've got my one over there and I've got my iPhone over here, I've got my Mac here and my PC over there and I've got three screens in front of me, and I've got lots of distractions.

None of those are turned on apart from the two screens that I need in order to conduct this call and to take messages from the team that is helping me present it.

That's the only thing I've got running at the moment because if you do this on the computer you will get distracted and you'll get that "You've got mail" alert and all that sort of thing.

Really don't do that. Turn everything off. Turn the wife off, turn the kids off, turn the husband off, turn the television off...turn everything off.

Do this separately. Completely away from everybody else. If you want to, grab a couple pieces of paper, grab a pencil, get in the car, drive out to your favourite place and do it there, because you won't get distracted.

Why write this down by hand? Well, two things happen. Number one, your subconscious mind becomes more engaged because it's your subconscious mind that holds the storyline that you're going to write down, and number two, your conscious, logical mind also becomes engaged because it's got to remember that symbol that looks like a fat man walking is actually an "R" and the fat man standing still is actually a "P." And the man standing with both his arms in the air is a "Y" and so on and so forth. So, the connection then between the two is very important.

I must admit that the first time I did this I did do it on a computer, but I did it on a computer with everything else turned off. And I know that Jane did hers on a computer. I'm just suggesting that it would be better if you didn't do that unless you are REALLY REALLY strict with yourself and the only thing you've got running on that computer and the only thing that you've got anywhere near you is that text editor.

And use a text editor. Don't use a big fancy program that can do all fancy stuff because this isn't about getting fancy. This is about getting to basics.

If you're wondering, "What the hell has this got to do with covert hypnosis?" what you've got to realize is that hypnosis is – and this isn't covert hypnosis – this is about persuasion. This is about inspiring people. This is about communication – and hypnosis is just a way of describing communication with the subconscious mind.

When we communicate with somebody's subconscious mind, and we get their subconscious mind wanting the same things we want, their subconscious mind will knock down every obstacle that has ever been put up in the way to get there. And THAT is what we want to achieve! Especially if we make that an enjoyable process for their subconscious mind.

So, it's all about the subconscious, and it's all about *their* subconscious, and this is how you get in rapport. This is how your conscious and your subconscious will get to know you better than you ever thought possible. And they'll stop fighting over you.

# The Core Rapport Process

You are going to write down your Typical Perfect Day

Notice that I say "typical." This is your *typical* perfect day. This isn't the day you go out and buy the Ferrari. This isn't the day you go out and impress a 19-year-old girl. This isn't the day you go out and pick up the Adonis. This isn't the day that you go out and win the prize and get the cup. This isn't the day that you go out and achieve climbing the mountain. This is a typical day.

This is the day that could be – I don't know if you've seen the film – but this could be your "Groundhog Day." This is the day that you could live over and over and over again and be perfectly happy. Be wonderfully, supremely happy. So it's not so much about things – it's about events.

I'll give you a bit of an idea in a minute by giving you bits of mine. But up until then, what I want you to do is just think about: "Forget the 'stuff,' forget the goals, forget everything else…what would my perfect day be if there are no limits at all?" That means no monetary limits and to a point no physical limitations in as much as you are not limited by health, you know…you're in the best health you could possibly be. There are no limits apart from the obvious.

Now let's face it. You cannot at this moment in time walk barefoot on the ceiling. You cannot, if you're a man, actually give birth. (You could gestate a foetus; it has been done, so somebody told me. I don't believe a word of it, but I suppose it is possible nowadays for them to connect everything up right and everything.) But you couldn't give birth. You still couldn't do that.

And if you don't own a space rocket and you are not an astronaut, you're not going to walk on the moon. So that probably won't be your typical day.

When I heard the marketer Frank Kern doing something like this, as he said, being in the Ferrari with four ladies of ill repute and three quarters of a kilo of crack is probably not going to be your perfect *typical* day. In fact after three quarters of a kilo of crack there probably won't be any more days!

So don't pick anything that will hurt you, harm you, get you into trouble, or something that you really can't do. You know me guys – I am completely and absolutely centred around the truth.

And I don't believe that if you can think it you can do it, because you might be able to think and you might be able to imagine that you can jump out of a plane with no parachute and fall three hundred thousand feet and bounce. Ain't gonna happen. Sorry. I don't care how good you are at manifesting or anything else. That is going to result in splat!

I know this is obvious. But it's not obvious to your subconscious mind because your subconscious mind actually has no limits. I'm engaging your conscious mind here. I know it's going against all the rules.

All the rules say that you must not have limits in place, but that's bollocks! It's complete and utter trash. It's crap. Because all that does is allow your subconscious mind to run and you get no congruence.

You get no inner rapport because your subconscious mind is going to come up with all these wonderful, marvellous, fabulous things that you can make people do when you learn these influence skills, and then at the end of it, when you haven't been able to do that, and you haven't been able to convince the person to try and walk up the wall (which you can do if they're hypnotized in other ways, but for this I don't want you to think you can do that), and even though you can convince people that they can walk on the ceiling, they can't do it. So to generate real Core Rapport in this exercise, there are no limitations except the obvious ones like the laws of physics.

What you're going to do, you're going to write down your perfect average day, your "Groundhog Day." I want you to do this in four parts. There is no structure to this as such. These are four elements that I want you to include, but don't do them in order. Don't do them in a way so that one necessarily follows the other. But make sure that as you are writing it down, they are all joined together.

I've got to warn you, that if you are the predictive type, or if you've especially had an emotional background, which most of us have (I come from a place where operations for all sorts of physical health issues have been a bit of a pain in the backside for me – we all come from emotional stuff), I want you to think on the future and not on the past.

21

In fact, close all the doors from the past. It happened, it's gone. Please, on your perfect day, don't include, "I'll be able to ride a bike again" when you've had something like rectal cancer and it's impossible to sit on a bike again. (Where do I get these things from?)

If you include something from the past, then you're just going to bring that conflict with you. Don't do that. This is the future. It's a completely clean slate. You can be anything and you can do anything you want within reason and within your obvious limits.

Of course, if you're in your fifties like me and you say, "Right, this is going to last three hundred years," you are probably going to fail!

## The four parts:

**Where**: describe your environment, where the things happen. Describe it in detail and let your mind create these wonderful places where your perfect day happens, and the places that you are living in.

**What**: describe what happens, what you are doing. Describe it in detail. Don't just say, "Oh, I woke up." Actually, my perfect day starts by saying:

*"I'm lying in a fantastic electronically positional bed that is in my huge en-suite bedroom in the house that Jane and I have just finished building, and I wake up in the morning and stretch."*

I'm describing my environment, I'm describing what I do – I wake up in the morning, I stretch – and I really am looking forward to this beautiful day because I just know it's going to be another experience that I am going to get SO much out of and is going to be enjoyed so much. So that's the next thing…

**Why**: describe why you are doing it. I wake up and I stretch and I'm so going to enjoy the day, I feel a sense of excitement rushing through me as I just know that things are going to be happening today that are going to make me feel really good.

**Result**: describe how it makes you feel with as much emotion as possible – the more emotion you put into it the better.

"Where" is a very logical thing. "What," also a very logical thing. "Why?" Emotional. "Result?" Also emotional. Now we are building congruence between your subconscious mind and your conscious mind. And if you do anything at all, or if you learn anything at all that doesn't get you into the right emotional state, then you are going to miss out. Now I'm not saying that you're going to fail, but it's going to be hard work.

Later on I'll be talking about rapport and about building rapport, and how to build rapport with other people, how to make friends with people.

We're not talking about rapport in the Neurolinguistic way or the "sales" way. We're talking about rapport in the *real* way, because rapport is what happens, as I said before, when two people or things are congruent with each other and moving in the same direction at the same speed going toward the same result. And that's what we're going to end up with.

So, you write down your typical day. You write down where, what, why, and result. And the next thing you need to know is that detail is vital. DETAIL IS VITAL. I can't tell you enough: *detail is vital*! The more detail you go into the more you are going to get out of this. The more detail you put in, the more detail comes out the other end.

What do you get out of this? This reveals your core self's desires and values, your core beliefs. These are not your ultimate goals or even the stuff you want. This isn't the conscious stuff at all that you've been doing for years and years and years. This is the stuff that hides behind and below everything else.

How many times have you thought to yourself, "I would really like that thing" and something's happened to stop you from getting it? Have you ever wondered why? I'll tell you why now: because no matter how much logical sense it makes for you to have that thing, your subconscious – your *core self* – doesn't believe that's what you should have.

Finding your core self isn't about finding out what's wrong with you so you can "cure" it. It's not about forgiving yourself. It's about understanding that your inner self wants stuff. And it's your conscious mind saying, "Well actually that makes sense. Okay, I'll go with that."

What's happened to me since I did this is I've started to notice that it's okay to be spiritual, for instance. I was blocking that off – I had sort of dipped into it and that sort of thing, but when I did dip into it I was thinking about psychic stuff and realizing that my spirituality goes in a totally different way from the way I was trying to put it, because I was trying to put it in a logical way and it doesn't work like that for me. So, I've become more feeling about those things.

But also, most importantly, I now know instinctively who I like most, and the sort of people I like most – the sort of people I want to talk to, the sort of people I want to deal with. And that's why all the people on the original course I did for this system were the sort of people who could get up off their asses and do something about their lives because if they weren't then they shouldn't have been involved. They're the sort of people who don't mind the odd "fuck" when I put it in (because I gratuitously swear) and they're the sort of people who really do want – and you really do want to make the most out of your life and everyone around you – and that's the most important thing.

As you're learning these things, if you are thinking about doing these for your evil whims and your evil ways, can you use it that way? Of course you can. But I'm warning you now, if you do, you're gonna get slapped. Not by me, but you're going to get slapped because that inner conflict is going to come back as soon as your conscious mind figures out that what you're doing is wrong in terms of the social world. You'll start to feel guilty, and as soon as you start to feel guilty you're going to have that conscious-/subconscious fight going on again, that conflict going on again, and you're going to feel crap. So please, get on with it. You won't really hurt anyone with it, by God. You are really going to feel the bad effects of it if you use it for the bad stuff.

25

Okay. I'll just run you through a quick recap. Step one of intent is that being in rapport with others is hard work unless you are in rapport with yourself. As soon as you get in rapport with yourself all the hard work just goes out the window and you relax and you become charismatic, you become charming, you become whatever it is you want to be.

Your typical perfect day – your typical, TYPICAL perfect day – this is the day that I'm saying, "If I turn this day on, you could live this day for eternity, so don't put anything in there that you wouldn't want to be in there for eternity.

It's in four parts:

- **Where** – describe your environment

- **What** – describe what you're doing

- **Why** – describe why you're doing it

- **Result** – describe how that makes you feel

And the detail is absolutely vital. This is going to reveal your core self's desires and values – not your ultimate goals, or even the stuff you want (or worse still, the stuff you think you should want) but your core self's desires and values. And that's because it's going to work your conscious and your subconscious mind in harmony. This is laying the foundations for everything else you're going to do.

I know people are reading this thinking, "Well, this is going to tell me how to go into a pub and get free drinks." It will. Trust me. If that's what you want to do with it. Of course, personally I can think of doing much better things with this, although I must admit that I was the only one that wasn't paying for tea in the last course that I ran. Fitzroy, the bartender thought I was a wonderful person (and he was right, I am. I'm just a wonderful person!)

So, run through this. Do it. Spend those few hours. When you have done this, sleep on it. Read it through as you are doing it. Don't read it again, don't read it anymore, don't share it with anybody, don't do anything with it at first – just put it in a drawer and sleep on it.

This allows your subconscious mind to get to know the core you. It allows your conscious mind in the morning when you wake up to be fed the stuff that it needs to know in order to know the core you, and it allows the whole thing to make friends.

This will put you in Core Rapport.

Once you know *you*, your goals become so bleeding obvious, it's incredible. If you are wondering, "Well, what do I actually want?" You will find out. Sleep on it for a day or two. And this will allow your subconscious mind to get to know who you really are – quite possibly for the first time in your life.

It may just be that you're already living your perfect day and your perfect lifestyle – and I know most of you aren't. We've all got things that aren't quite right. Mine isn't perfect by any means yet, but I'm moving rapidly toward that now because I've done the Core Rapport and am in rapport with myself, so I'm doing stuff now that is moving there faster than I have ever done in my whole life! So trust me on this one. This will work.

I can't reiterate the strength of getting the tools, which are your mind and your brain – the tools that you're going to be using to influence, to persuade, to install in others the desire to want to make you happy and give you what you want (because the reward to them is going to be so great), so you can tell where this is going. I really can't impress on it, though, the absolute need for you to have this solid basis.

I know there are probably some people who are thinking, "I'd rather not go here." It isn't like that at all. It isn't like finding out whether what you did was good bad, or whether it was installed by an evil grandparent or a father or mother – it's not about that at all, because all of that's a pile of poo as well! (I would say that it's a lump of shit, but I've been told I shouldn't swear as much. I like the word "profanity," though, and sometimes I profane too much.)

It's not about finding out what you've been doing wrong because the only thing you've been doing wrong is that you've been living your life in conflict. It's about finding out what your Core Rapport is and teaching both parts of you, both of your mental processes — the actual thing that is you, the original being that is you – what this "you" is moving toward.

So it isn't about finding out what you've done bad because you've done nothing bad.

You've done absolutely nothing wrong! And the only reason that your life hasn't been wonderful and hasn't been moving to where you want it to go is because of that internal combustion and internal conflict. And that's going to end over the next few days.

# The Secret of True Intent

As a Hypnotist I teach Hypnotists that the most vital thing is the **intent of the hypnotist.**

If you're working with somebody you can't stand, somebody you think is a dickhead and they ought to give themselves a shake and get on with it, you are not going to have a success there. You may have a *technical* success in a one-to-one room, but that person will go away and they will, within days, be a failure. You won't have that intent in place. You won't have that "I know exactly what's going to happen with you and how far it's going to go."

Now, let's say that one day I'm coaching a guy named Jeff over the phone. I happen to know that if it is my intent to stick Jeff to his chair à la Derren Brown or sticking his hand to the telephone à la me, that's doable. That's possible because I know that Jeff is in deep rapport with me because he wants as much out of this as I want him to have out of this.

So if my intent was that way, then that would occur, regardless of Jeff's conscious state, regardless of his trance state or anything like that, because if I put that into place there would be absolutely no doubt in my mind that this would be the result I would have.

That's where intent comes into it.

You may have heard of the Law of Attraction and attracting stuff and manifesting stuff. And it says that you've got to get your mind right. What you've really got to have is the lack of doubt. There must be absolutely no room for doubt.

What a lot of the systems tell you to do is to point your intent at the target. "It's my intent for that target to put his hand in his pocket and buy me lunch." Great. Fabulous.

Now, how does he get there? Which pocket? Is his wallet in his pants pocket of his jeans? Is he wearing jeans? Is it in his suit jacket? The inside pocket? Is it on a money belt? Where is it?

How the hell can you figure all that out beforehand?

You can't, so you go in with a loose idea that he's just going to pay for your lunch in some fashion. The problem that I have with this is, for me, it's not detailed enough. It's just not detailed enough.

Let's go back to that example of Jeff being on the phone with me. Now, maybe he'd be on a headset, but I would know that a phone would be involved, so I could tell him to pick up the handset, right? I know that, so my intent could be inclined to stick his hand to the handset. But I don't do it that way.

I do it by dealing with *me* – not the target. That's right. When I'm doing intent, when I'm going in to a situation, into a hypnotic situation, into an influence situation, I target *myself*, not the target. I know for sure, for absolutely certain, how I want to feel. I know what I'm going to be wearing. I know where my wallet's going to be. I know the situation I'm going to be in. It's a hell of a lot easier

31

to target *me* as the end result than it is to target *somebody else* as the end result.

Sitting there in my jeans and denim shirt and jean jacket and sitting back in the chair feeling well-fed and knowing that I haven't paid for a damn thing that I've eaten or drank makes me feel really marvellous. It makes me feel so good and so full of gratitude that I've got toward the person who bought me lunch, that I'm just going to feel absolutely great.

Now, here's the important thing. Say I was in a social situation with six or seven people. I could go out with the intention that this one's going to buy me lunch or that one's going to buy me lunch or that one's going to buy me lunch, and that starts to get silly.

But if I've got the intent and lack of doubt that I'm going to sit back having had lunch bought for me, one of those people is going to buy. I don't know which one, and to be quite honest I don't care because I'm not targeting them. I'm targeting me.

This is a highly generalized situation. And I know it doesn't fit well with what a lot of people reading this who might think, "Well, this isn't what I want to use this for because in a sales situation I'd have to be more specific." Yes, you'd have to be more specific on yourself. Not on somebody else. It's easier to intend the way we feel than it is to intend the way other people feel.

What amazes me over and over and over again is that I have read that the first thing you do is get into rapport. The second thing you do is to force, cajole, or persuade someone to do what you want them to do. If you are in rapport, they want to do what you want anyway!

If you are absolutely and vitally clear on what you want to feel – and remember, you're in Core Rapport now so what you want to feel in that situation is so clear – and you go into that situation, then once you're in rapport (and you're going to be in rapport because your Core Rapport is going to help you get there) you don't have to do very much to get that person to want what you want.

Go back to the soccer match. Go back to the football match. When you get back to the people being in rapport even though they want to kill each other, it's very simple and very easy. I used to do this time and time again.

I was a football hooligan and I used to stand there with all the home fans and you'd stand there and have twenty thousand people around you and you're all in rapport.

Somebody would shout out the name of the team and clap their hands and before you knew what was happening there would be twenty thousand people doing that! That's real rapport. They all wanted to do the same thing as you because it made them feel good for the same reasons.

So, remove doubt – be absolutely positive about where you're going and how you feel, and they will just come with you. They will have no bloody choice because the only way they're going to feel as good as you feel **is** to go with you!

If you don't have Intent then it's a bit like standing in that crowd of football fans, and being the only person who's not chanting the name of the team. Not only are you going to feel pressure, or almost guilt, but you're going to become very conspicuous. If you know what you want, then you will find that you won't be standing in the middle of people who don't want what you want. You won't even be at the football match!

Your subconscious mind won't put you in that situation. You will be working all these things on automatic! Look at your receptacle. Just in your mind's eye…I know it's there. It can't *not* be there. I've installed it! Do you think you had a choice on whether that receptacle was in your head or not? And you may say, "Oh, I'm not visualizing anything." But you can describe it to me, can't you?

But if you say, "Oh no, I can't describe it." Okay then, describe *any* receptacle to me…and that's the one I want. I am using the tools I am installing in you to teach you, and you have no choice. Isn't that terrible? Because I know that at the end of this, I want you guys to feel the same as me, and you want to feel the same as me: that this is just the best thing since sliced bread!

I'm being so underhanded with this aren't I…so covert. But this is exactly the way I would do it in a social situation, exactly the way I'd do it in a business situation, and those of you who have trained with me know that this is exactly the way I do it in a training situation. And it's exactly the way I do it in relationships.

In just a minute I'm just going to give you a little test. I've given this to some of you before, but I'm just going to give you a little test just to show you how much people work in conflict, but on a subconscious level. And I'll give you that as a freebie in just a little while.

But before that, the secret to true intent is to target yourself, not the target. You know for sure how you want to feel. You remove doubt – and this is the secret – you remove doubt by disregarding the unpredictable.

## Disregarding The Unpredictable

As I said, all the other things that tell you to go into detail like "Oh this person's going to give me lunch, and he's going to feel good about that" and the rest – all of that's unpredictable. How *you're* going to feel, what *you're* going to be wearing, everything that you can visualize, if you can visualize, all the detail that you are absolutely sure will be there.

And by the way, if you think you can't visualize, you can. Try visualizing with your eyes open. There is no such thing as a person who can't run a visual program. What I get with people who can't visualize is that if you ask them to visualize with their eyes open, they can do it fine. If you just close your eyes now as you are reading this and think, "Now what can I see?" The only thing you can actually see is the inside of your damned eyelids!

However, the visual cortex works whether your eyes are open or closed. But your logical brain doesn't. And the people who say they can't visualize are just the ones whose brain and mind are in conflict, because although the mind can run the idea of what visualization is absolutely, the conscious mind can't interpret that, and it doesn't make any sense at all to the conscious mind to be able to visualize with your eyes closed.

So if you're one of those people who say you can't visualize if you open your eyes and describe a picture to yourself, your mind and your brain will get more into coherence together and they will be able to describe that picture. That's running exactly the same pattern as everybody else, just interpreting that in a different way.

When I say visualize the results, you can visualize. Most people, when they're trying to visualize results, when they're trying to get the intent right, when they're trying to get that right, they visualize the other person or they try to visualize a situation where they can see themselves in the other person. And that's all totally and completely and absolutely wrong because you're creating internal conflict, because your conscious mind doesn't know what it's like to step outside of itself and imagine a situation where it can see itself.

The only way your conscious mind and your conscious brain can see itself is to look in a mirror. Think about this. So look in a mirror while you're actually saying, "Yes I do feel pleased with myself. I feel really good. I do feel pleased with myself. I feel proud. I've done really well here." Use that Core Rapport!

Now don't worry about that at the moment. I only tell people to do that thing in the mirror if they haven't done the Core Rapport, because once you've done the Core Rapport you will not have the internal conflict anymore! If there's not that internal conflict, then you quite simply go into a situation knowing completely and absolutely and logically that this is going to happen. That's intent: no doubt.

I want to just finish off here with a quote, and I'm not sure where it comes from, and I changed it a bit. Rapport is the art of communicating – just like hypnosis is – with people in such a way that people are inspired to give you what you want. I'll repeat that. Rapport is the art of communicating with people in such a way that they are inspired to give you want you want.

\*\*\*\*\*\*\*\*\*\*\*\*\*\*\*\*\*\*\*\*\*\*\*\*\*\*\*\*\*\*\*\*\*\*\*\*\*\*\*\*\*\*\*\*\*\*\*\*\*\*

Note: I believe this a quote from Marshal Sylver - but don't quote me on it!

Now there's absolutely no comeback on this either is there? They're not going to come back two days later and say, "Oh, well, you got me to do that and you convinced me to buy lunch, and you bastard, you never bought me lunch, and I'm not going out with you again!" And that's what's going to happen if you just use this ad hoc, and you use it in situations where your stuff isn't actually what that person wants, and when your happiness isn't what that person wants.

Again, rapport is the art of communicating with people in such a way that they feel *inspired* to give you want you want.

So here's a quick recap:

The secret to true intent is to target yourself, not the target.

You are intending your feeling whatever it is you want to feel.

It's purely focused on you.

It's all about you.

Your whole life is about you!

It's not about other people.

It's about you.

Your intent is about YOU!

And that's fine! That's okay! That's great! It's wonderful to be selfish, because when you're coherent with yourself, and when you're in rapport with yourself, what you want for yourself is as much fun, as much enjoyment, as much enlightenment, as much knowledge, as much feeling of every day being perfect as you can possibly have it – and when you want that, think of the people in history who have actually had that. There was no conflict, it wasn't causing anybody else any harm, and you see that you've got some pretty wonderful people, and some pretty rich and pretty un-screwed-up people on that list.

On the other hand, you can keep your conflict. Providing you've got your conflict, you won't be able to get intent, you won't be able to get Core Rapport, you won't be able to get awe rapport, you won't be able to get rapport with other people, you will not build up rapport, you can put these tools to use and they will work only with about twenty percent of people. And I want to get you to have this working with eighty percent.

# CLASS 1

## ACTION SECTION

Intent - Know what you want to achieve

# Intent and your Core Rapport

The first CLASS in the Svengali System deals with Intent. The key to this phase of the system is finding out exactly what it is you want to achieve to get rid of doubt. The end result will be that you will find people are more inspired to give you what you want when you need it because you will be acting and thinking totally differently and with more charisma and influence!

The main concept you will see mentioned throughout the Svengali System is **Core Rapport.** Obviously, you are familiar with the word rapport.

However, this word is not used very often outside of the hypnosis NLP and Marketing and sales industries. So what does it mean exactly? If you look the word rapport up in the dictionary, you will see it defined as "relation marked by harmony, conformity, accord, or affinity."

For our purposes here, we can break this definition down even further. Rapport means empathy and resonance, in short it means friendship. You want to form a level of friendship with whomever you are communicating with. More importantly you want to achieve rapport with yourself.

**Why Rapport?**

Rapport is crucial to the Svengali System. You want the person you are influencing, let's call them the Influencee, to have two main things in common with you.

These two things are:

1) Desires and goals

2) Principals and perspective

**Keep It Simple**

Keep in mind, that simplicity is ok. In fact, if you have any issues with keeping things as simple as possible, please release that resistance. The Svengali System is all about simplicity.

Everything we do should be fun and easy. After all, we are dealing with your subconscious, and your subconscious has an outlook similar to that of a child

> *"Complexity is hard work. Work smart... if you work at all." –* Jonathan Chase

**Your Subconscious- A Bright 9 Year Old Child**

It's important to begin viewing your subconscious as a bright 9-year-old child. Everything should be easy and accessible to your subconscious. When you give your subconscious (or anyone else's subconscious) suggestions and instructions, these need to be oriented for a bright 'smart' 9 year old.

Just like a 9 year old, your subconscious will not understand anything that is too complicated.

## Facts about 9 Year Olds

—Up until the age of 9, the brain isn't mature enough to get in the way. We are emotive, creative and just want what we want. We make choices based on desire as opposed to reason.

—This time period is one before our views and understanding of logic truly sets in.

—Around the age of 9, our brain matures and mature sociological neural pathways are formed. At this point, logic is primed to take over.

Your subconscious is at this level of development. It matches all the criteria listed above.

In fact, most of the time when you make decisions, it's based on the logic of a 9 year old! This last sentence isn't meant as an insult to you. It's just a fact that most of our decisions are made based on emotions and free of logic. We want to follow what feels good; similar to the way a child would make decisions.

For example, children see a commercial of something on TV that looks great and they get excited. They tell their parents, "I want that!" Haven't you also had that experience where you decide to buy something based on how it will make you feel? Actually you Always make your buying decisions that way.

Kids learn best at play and having fun. We want your head full of dopamine. Dopamine is a neurotransmitter produced in the brain at times of true joy, excitement and fun. These are all emotions that a 9 year old can easily access. That is also the state that your subconscious is attracted to and seeks to access because this is the feel good drug. (And it's also totally free!)

# 3 Factors to Reach the Subconscious

## It must be easy
## It must be fun
## It must be effective

# The First Step...
# Your Own Core Rapport

It is time to create your own core rapport and get to be friends with the most important person in your life. You may be wondering 'Why am I creating my own core rapport? Isn't this all about influencing other people?'

The fact of the matter is that **being in rapport with others is hard work, unless you are in rapport with yourself.** And I'm presuming you hate hard work as much as I do. And if it's hard you're doing it wrong!

As soon as you connect and are aware with your true self, you will automatically begin to become "attractive" and irresistible to others. And it's the people we find attractive and likable that have the greatest influence over us.

Once you know these facts, you'll know the perfect types of people for you to seek out as potential clients, relationships, sources of cash, or whatever you may be seeking, and be able to inspire them to give you what you both need when you need it.

## Exercise: Create Your Typical Perfect Day

For this exercise, the first step is to take out pen and paper. Don't use your computer. If you are thinking you might just ignore this point, and use your computer anyway. Please don't.

One of the main points to this exercise is to access your subconscious mind. If you are on the computer, you will not be able to do this effectively. You will not focus. When we are on our computers, we are constantly distracted on some level by bright shiny stuff, evil voices announcing we have e-mail, Skype pings every time a buddy arrives or leaves. Turn everything off.

Now that you are off your computer, take some time to figure out what your core self wants by telling yourself the story of what it would be like to have it, and to have it for every Typical day for the rest of your life without limits other than these. There are no limits as regards cash, health, or where you are. This could be anywhere it is possible to live. Nothing on this day should harm you or others physically or emotionally. Nothing on this day should be monumental. 'One off stuff' that you would do only on unusual days is out.

Now set aside at least two hours, preferably take the whole day off and be on your own.

## BEGIN

## Step 1:

Sit down with your pen and paper in a quiet place where you won't be disturbed.

## Step 2: The Where

Now on paper describe this typical perfect day in as much detail as possible. Try to put as many specifics into this description as possible. Be sure to make your description rich with detail.

This is not necessarily the environment you are in now; it is the perfect one you are moving towards so it doesn't have to be one you are familiar with yet.

'My bedroom is 60square feet. The lush thick green rug under the huge super sized bed ends to reveal the buffed and warm solid oak floorboards.'

## Step 3: The What

Describe what you are doing on this day. Remember, this is not what you *could* be doing. You are describing what you are actually doing. Write it as if you are there and again detail. 'I wake up and sit up.' 'I brush my teeth.'

It is best here to give yourself a timing as well. 'It's seven thirty.'

## Step 4: The Why

Describe why you are doing what you do. There is a reason behind all your motivations. They could be "because it makes me feel good," or perhaps "because it makes them feel good." Perhaps you do what you do because it moves you toward a certain goal.

Give the why some thought and add this to your description

## Step 5: The Result

Describe how you now feel that you are living your perfect day. For example, "I feel calm and warm doing...."

## REMEMBER

**Point 1:** There are no limits on the day, apart from the obvious. Don't include things in the day that you know are impossible. For example, being immortal, flying, turning invisible etc. should not be in your perfect day description. Otherwise, you will have some level of conflict and disharmony in your description.

**Point 2:** This is a **typical** perfect day. So your description shouldn't include things that can only happen once.

Keep in mind this is a day that happens on a repetitive basis. This would be your groundhog day; a day you could be stuck in with a bloke called Murray and not get bored or go la-la. So your **typical** perfect day can't include items like getting a Ferrari, meeting the queen, attending a crack orgy.

The more detail and description you include, the faster you will truly make contact with our core self. Once you truly understand who you are and what you want, you will be able to release your doubt.

> When describing your perfect day, Detail is VITAL! Emotion is VITAL!

## Step 6: Sleep on It

Once you have finished writing down your perfect day, put the

---

SECRET OF TRUE INTENT = LACK OF DOUBT

---

paper or notepad, if you're like me, in a drawer near your bed. Stop looking at it. Then go to sleep. This process allows your subconscious to get to know the core you.

Your subconscious will make friends with these elements while you are sleeping.

To become Influential you MUST have an exact target of what it is you want to create for yourself and for the Influencee. We call this Intent.

### Target Yourself, Not the Other Person

The most vital thing is the Intent of the hypnotist. This process of finding your typical perfect day reveals your core self's desires and values.

When you deal with intent initially, you target yourself. Don't seek to target the other person. Once you have established your perfect day and understand your core self, you understand important factors about yourself. Remember it is not about the other person entirely. It is about you.

Remove doubt by disregarding the unpredictable. You cannot predict another person's behaviour or the environment entirely. However, you can predict your own to the point where you act as if you have already achieved what you needed and wanted to achieve.

Without doubt you will be projecting true self- confidence. As a result, other people will want to come along for the ride.

Once you are in rapport with yourself, you don't have to do much to get someone to do what you want and feel great about their wanting to do it. They will have no choice. After all, they will feel that the easy way they can feel good, is to come along with you!

"Influence is mastering the art of communicating with people in such a way as they are inspired to give you what you both need and want."

## Summary

### Step one of true Intent

—Target yourself not the 'target'.

### Step two of intent.

—Once you have identified your perfect day and made contact with your core self, you know for sure how you want to feel. Remove doubt by disregarding the unpredictable.

# CLASS 2

Attracting the Right People
Presupposition - Games and Experiments
Giving People Stuff - Observation
Parrot Rapport and the Big Question Mark

# Attracting the Right People

I hope you have done your Core Rapport. You should have done your Core Rapport by now. Now the Core Rapport is very important to get into with yourself because automatically that will help you get your intent right. And remember, intent is about focus and it's about a lack of doubt. And lack of doubt can be seen as confidence, can't it?

If you notice, I did say that I would be "installing" this. And when I did this as a live course I got phone calls and emails saying, "Hey, without even thinking about it my confidence has gone through the roof and my focus has improved!" Yes, that is going to happen because that's the whole idea of installing this!

These things are going to happen because I'm actually putting them into your subconscious mind. How am I doing that? Well, we are going to talk a little bit about how we will be getting that sort of rapport.

Before we do that, though, I want to give you one extra use for your Core Rapport that's just going to change the way you work. I was watching a video on Youtube that was all about persuasion and influence and it was saying how you have to sell yourself to people and it's all about selling yourself to people. I look at it this way: you shouldn't have to *sell* yourself to people if they are the right people! You shouldn't have to say, "Look at me, I'm wonderful, I'm marvellous." If they are the right people they are already going to **know** that!

So how do you find the right people? How do you know that you're going to be attracting the right people? It's important that you become attractive and start attracting people.

I know a lot of these things state that when you go into a social situation that you may be in there with a lot of people that you don't like and all that blah blah blah blah blah, and you should be able to manipulate those people in order to get them to like you, but that is a very shallow and very thin veneer of friendship, because the moment you walk out of the room, that goes.

I'll talk in a little bit about making friends, not enemies. But, if you are in Core Rapport, you will start to not only attract the right sort of people that you can move toward the place that they need to go a lot easier (*manipulate* is probably not quite the right word because what you are doing here is **steering!** ), not only will you attract them, but you become attractive to them, and that builds up rapport again.

We're going to talk about that. And later on I'm going to talk about awe rapport and how to install that, because it is important. And we're going to talk about giving people stuff. And we're going to talk about observing people and watching for the passion and the wistfulness and even their sadness.

But the first thing that I want you to do is to go through your Core Rapport thing again, but this time not for you. If you are in business and you are looking for clients, I want you to do this with your clients. If you are looking for a relationship, I want you to do this with potential partners. If you are looking at becoming more inspirational to your family, I want you to do it for your family.

However, families are slightly different because, unfortunately, families are a lot more to do with genetics and chance than they are to do with choice. But we can still get into a position where even then we become more attractive to people.

Let's start with clients. Most people who are taking this course or reading this book are in a business situation. They're looking for clients, they're looking for maybe joint ventures, or maybe looking for making partnerships with people, they're looking to sell stuff to people, they're looking to inspire people to buy stuff, or looking for people to inspire to buy their stuff.

The easiest way to find the right client is just run a Core Profile on them. What is your client's name? Are they male or female? And please don't say, "Well, they could be both," because if you do that, you immediately lose focus because they could be both. Then you'll start saying, "Well they could be this type of person or that type of person or the other type of person."

Do the Core Profile and go into detail. What do your clients want? I'll tell you that ultimately they want the same thing as you. And if you get what you want down to playtime, if you get what you want down to freedom, if you get what you want down to security, the chances are that your clients will want exactly the same thing.

It's no huge stretch of the imagination to take this into relationships, is it? In fact, it's much more important in relationships, because these are the people you are going to have around you forever. (Although hopefully your clients are as well.) In social relationships, it's almost inevitable that you are going to attract people who want the same things that you do. Not only do they want the same things as you, but surprise, surprise, they're using the exact same methods to get those things!

If they're looking for excitement and your way of looking for and finding excitement is to jump out of an airplane with a piece of silk tied to your back at thirty thousand feet, then the chances are the people you will be attracting will be the same sort of idiots! Err, I mean the same sort of people who like that sort of exciting pastime!

Running a Core Profile on your typical – *typical* – average client will give you focus because as soon as you start to do that you realize where they are and who they are and they become incredibly easy to find.

Think about it from a dating point of view. If you're looking for somebody, what do you do? You just go out to a singles bar and you hang around and you hope that somebody who looks nice might start talking to you or you'll start doing the pickle party stuff and you'll start talking to them. Again, the only problem is that it does tend to be very shallow and short lived. It's great if you're looking for a quick overnighter, but it's not much use if you're looking for solid, ongoing relationships. Ultimately it's empty.

And it's the same with clients. Anybody can sell anything to anybody. You can force people to buy. And that's great. That's fabulous. And I'll tell you I used to do that. I used to be in a situation where I forced people to buy stuff. And they would buy it and they would go away and a couple of weeks later they would either come back knocking on the door or they would email me or even going further before email (yes, I was alive before email), people used to write me letters and say, "Look, this stuff is actually crap."

That may or may not have been because the stuff was actually crap. I liked the stuff, certainly, but it was because they didn't want it in the first place and after a while they realized that they just didn't want it.

A lot of these covert conversational persuasive, influential techniques are based on that old model of selling. You know, you force people to think what you want them to think. You take them into where they don't want to be, and make them or cajole or manipulate them into doing something they didn't want to do in the first place, so there's no result in it for them.

It's so bad that here in the UK you have a thirty day opt-out. No matter what contract or sale you take out with anybody else in the United Kingdom, you have a thirty-day opt-out. For example, I bought a Wii gaming system because they're fabulous and they're great and it's a boy's toy and I love boy's toys, and most of my clients love boy's toys in some way. When I bought it, they told me that there's a thirty day opt-out on the thing even though I'd been in the shop, I picked the thing out, I looked at it, I had taken it away, I can use it, and if I take it back within thirty days I can just cancel that contract and it stops.

The same thing happens in covert hypnosis stuff. If you are looking for instant gratification and satisfaction, then using the methods I'm teaching you are no problem. But then again, I'm telling you that there is absolutely no point whatsoever at all in doing it that way. It's a waste of time.

What's the use of having a client or relationship that goes away within thirty days? You want clients that not only are going to come back to you, but they feel so much like friends, they recommend other people to you. It's the old sales thing: people buy from people they **know, like, and trust**. And we know, like, and trust our friends. So don't be a salesman, whatever you do.

Doing the Core Profile means that you don't have to be a salesman because you're both going in the same way. And what happens then is you are going to be in a situation as far as your client is concerned where you say, "I know where you're going because I'm going in the same direction. Let me show you how to get there." That's when the sale takes place because they want to go to the same place, and they turn around and say, "Thank you very much!"

You've actually given them something of value, and they will show their appreciation by giving you something of value, which, in most cases in the world the way it is today, is cash – money.

Moving on from clients to social relations – and as I said, we want those to hang around as well. We don't want them necessarily to give us money, but what we do want them to be is comfortable in our presence so that they share existence with us. And that's really where a relationship comes from.

And you know, lots and lots of relationships are based on shallower things. Certainly if you apply these methods, you can use these methods just to get laid. And about the methods, which we'll get more and more into as the book goes on, don't be impatient because the setup and understanding are so important. If we didn't do it this way it would be a bit like learning to read, but not learning what the words mean, and saying "cat" but having no picture in your head of that nice little four-legged fiend that lives with you rather than you living with it. You must have the understanding first, and that's what the Core Rapport things are about.

So anyway, you can use these methods just to get laid. No problem at all, very simple and very easy. In fact, that's much easier than building up a fulfilling, long-term relationship most of the time. Because with long-term relationships you have to get yourself into a situation where you're attracting the right people.

And I like saying to people, "How do you know you're in the right relationship?" Well, it works like this: is your partner your best friend? They should be. And it's the same with your clients. They should be your best friends. They should be the people that you are quite happy to see.

We've had an ex-client of mine who is now a partner in the business, and his wife and child spend the weekend with us, and we'll have a great time hanging out, and we'll go to see penguins on the English Riviera (not free ones, admittedly, since they're in a zoo thing at Living Coasts), and we went and did stuff and had a fabulous Sunday lunch and that sort of thing, and that was great! But that only happens because I make friends of my clients, and that's vitally important.

It's the same in social relations. So you're looking to get laid. Great. But it's way better to do that with someone who's going to be around afterward than it is to wake up in the morning and find they're gone and you've got to go through all of it again. So if you want to use these methods for that fine. No problem. But personally, I would suggest that you don't because it's just going nowhere.

Your family – now this is a hard one. It's always the hard one. The reason it's the hard one is that we don't get to choose, do we? Unfortunately, we don't get to find our family – we get to suffer them most of the time.

So how do we get into a situation where we can help them become more – not like we wish them to be, but how can we help them find their experience and enhance that?

One of the big problems with families is of course that temptation to create the person we would like them to be. With our children, unfortunately, we tend to do that. We certainly create the people that they become, and that may not always be the person we want them to be, but we certainly put a lot of input into that. How can we get them so that we're moving in the same situation and direction, so that we can inspire them to give us what we need, whatever that may be?

The easiest way to do this is to run the Core Rapport on them and be absolutely, completely, and totally bloody honest. Certainly with your teenage kids that will probably not include you. But there are the rules. Remember the rules. If they are old enough, get them to do this themselves, but if not, their Core Rapport day should not include anything that would get them into trouble, and should not include anything that could be harmful to them or anybody else. Remember that. Nothing that's harmful to them or anyone else, and nothing with limitations.

For those who aren't home at the moment, forget that and do the Core Profile to really look at them for the first time. You should know your family well enough to know what they ultimately want. And once you find out what they ultimately want, you can help them move toward that. That may not be exactly the same as what you want, but hey – we can't all be the same can we?

Once you start to do that, and once you start to understand the people around you, certainly the people who are very close to you, you become more attractive and you start attracting more people. And the more people come into your life the more energy in the form of "stuff" that starts moving around in your life, and the more results to you on both an emotional and a physical level.

This is what I call working smart, not hard. Otherwise, if you don't do this, you're going to be working hard all the time. You'll be going into situations where you are guessing what people want and what people don't want.

What happens when you Core Rapport your perfect clients, when you Core Rapport your typical average clients or potential partner? What happens there is you will generally focus only on those people. The rest of the world will kind of go into that gray area on the sidelines.

Think of it as a sports game where you're on the pitch, and you've got twenty-two other players on there who are all playing the same game as you, and you can only see them. I know when I've worked with footballers it doesn't matter if there are sixty or seventy thousand people in the ground, they forget all about them because they focus down. Certainly they do when I've worked with them! They focus down on the twenty-two other players who are all in the same game. And it's taking that out, using the Core Profile, very simply and easily taking that out and putting it into the real world so that even if you're in a city with twenty million other people, it's only the few players that are in your game that you meet.

That puts your intent and your focus into a level that goes way beyond everybody else who is trying to make people who aren't attracted to them attracted to them. The number one step has gone out the window. You don't need to do that anymore! You're working smart, not hard.

It's like you will be putting your shop – and it doesn't matter whether you're selling a business or selling a product or selling yourself, or whether your selling your kids their future, it doesn't matter – you are putting your shop in exactly the right place without even having to look for the place. It all happens organically! You're working smart, not hard.

Sure I can talk you through words that can manipulate peoples' minds into buying. We've got the "yes" thing for example, although soon I'll be telling you about Absolute Truths, which we want people to be experiencing rather than some simple "yes" thing. It's not about getting someone to say "yes" seven times and then hitting them with a question because I'll tell you what – eighty percent of those people are going to come back and say, "I didn't want this. Give me my money back." And that is going to be the same situation no matter what it is you're selling. Remember – working smart, not hard.

If any of this stuff, as you are going through it or doing it in the real world starts to feel hard, stop. Don't do it anymore. It won't work because it will be that "thin veneer" thing that you're doing. So long as it's easy and so long as it feels easy, you're using your own emotions now as a gauge as to whether you're doing this right or not. As long as it feels easy and you're just breezing along with it, then you know that you're doing it right.

## A quick recap:

Core Profile your typical average target person. I don't care whether they are a client, whether they are a potential partner (be that sexual or social in some way) or even a member of your family. If you Core Profile them, you will understand them, you will know them, you will be thinking about them, you will be focusing on them.

Your whole body, and your whole being will move into that part of the playing pitch and you will attract and be attractive to the people who are going to be playing the same game as you. And that's important. They are playing the same game as you. And if they are playing the same game as you it isn't hard to play anymore.

# Presupposition:

I'm beginning this section with a blog I wrote when the question of presupposition came up on the membership pages on the interweb:

"There is a term used in NLP, Presupposition.

Before presupposition the French had a term for it which pre-dates presupposition by about a hundred years first appearing around 1845 in a history of a Franco army triumph.

The term?

Fait Accompli – which means 'the deed is done'. That roughly means to suppose that something has already happened.

Creating a reality as if it has already happened, even though it will happen in the future, is what hypnotists have been doing as a matter of course for a few hundreds of years and what subconscious minds have been doing for ever.

"When I wake you, you HAVE forgotten your name." The presupposition there is you **Have** forgotten it even though that hasn't happened yet.

What you DO with it is to act as if the result is a thing of the present rather than a thing of the future.

For instance to get someone to shut the door you could say, "Closing the door was a good idea."

Don't hide it, there is no need. Their brain won't understand it as it has no future nor past and becoming confused will give over control to the mind. Their mind will just believe it and to make it so and feel 'good' it Has To Shut The Door.

What will happen is they will look at you with a frown or even say "What?" and then they will close the door to 'feel good'.

Of course you could just say, "Please shut the door," but that isn't anywhere near as much fun as playing the mind game!

So to use a presupposition move your imagination into a place where Fait Accompli! And act and talk as if it is."

That leads me on to an NLP thing, and those of you who know me well know that I consider NLP a "Nauseatingly Lengthy Panto-mime" as Don McPherson the MindBender.co.uk, one of the members in one of my groups said; or **my** version of that is that it's hypnosis "Not Learned Properly!" But there is one interesting word and one useful thing that came out of NLP, and that's presupposition. And the next thing I wanted to talk to you about is presuppositions.

We're actually getting into the working of things now. By now you should have done **your Core Rapport**, you've done a Core Profile for your ideal client, you understand that what you're looking for is a lasting relationship with somebody, and you give them something of value and you get the value back, you get their appreciation back, and to inspire them. And you understand that it's about attracting and being attractive and being attracting. And it's easy to be attractive in a world where you are focusing on the people who are just like you, who you know very, very well, and who are moving toward the same goals as you.

You're working smart, not hard.

Presupposition. What is presupposition? It's presupposing something. It's assuming that something has already occurred.

When I was on stage as a stage hypnotist, one thing I always used to do was wait for my opening music to come on. It was quite dramatic and it used to say, "Fasten your seatbelts. Extinguish your cigarettes. Open your minds!" And while that was going on I would be at the side of the stage with my head bowed and my eyes closed and I would be running my presupposition. And that would be visualizing the audience going absolutely crazy at the end of the show. I would then go out and act as if that had already occurred.

In all the years that I was on stage in all the shows that I did, I never failed once to get volunteers on stage. Never. It never happened because of presupposition. Because I just knew that could never happen. I had difficult people occasionally who came up on stage and may not have been easy to hypnotize, and didn't go, but half of that was working with the old idea of *selling* them something – persuading them to come and do something.

And you'll see that a lot with stage hypnosis. You'll see people persuading people to come up on stage and then they go, "Uh, right, changed my mind. I don't like it up here so I'm packing up and going." And that's why we lose half of the people who come up on stage. They simply have been sold or manipulated to come up on stage and they just leave.

You don't want that to happen in your world. You don't want to have that happen with clients. You don't want to have that happen in social relationships where people just leave when they realize they've been manipulated. And it doesn't matter how good a manipulator you are, that will happen.

There's a rather famous film about a guy in Italy apparently hypnotizing some woman in some shop and taking money off her. But basically the most important thing to note is that the woman remembered that she'd given the guy some money. She didn't remember why she'd given the guy some money, but she did remember that she'd given them the money. And you will get caught if you're playing that game, so be very, very careful.

In presupposition you imagine that the thing is already done and dusted. If you're going into a situation where you want fantastic service, imagine that you've already had it. Virtually say "Thank you for the fantastic service that I've just had" to the person who is serving you before they even serve you.

Very easy, neat little trick, that. Because if you go into a situation believing that you've already had fantastic service, ninety-nine point nine percent of the time you will get perfect service. If you go into a situation thinking "I'm going to make friends here!" I'll guarantee it. If you go into a situation thinking that you're going to manipulate people into becoming your friends and you're going to build rapport and do all this fancy stuff, it won't happen.

An easy way to do this of course is what most really influential people do, they "Pre-tip". That is they give the person giving them service a tip before they get the service.

Presupposition is the most vital tool you have when you're going into a situation where you want to influence the end result. And remember that's what you're doing. You're going into a situation where you want to influence the end result.

I'm going to give you some words to use later that you'll be able to apply, but mostly, that's what we're talking about. Mostly we are talking about something that I hate to call "manipulation." When you say "manipulation" it's a bit like saying "paedophile," because people have all these things around manipulation, even though that's what we do all the time. It's what we all do to each other.

But from here on out I'm going to blatantly use the word *manipulation* all the time because all it means is moving something around. Moving things toward things or away from things. That's all manipulation means, and it's a perfect word for the situation.

I hate PC when it limits stuff from being understood simply. I call myself a cripple because that's what I am – physically anyway. Some people think I am a cripple emotionally and mentally as well. But one hopes not! Anyway, we're going to use the word *manipulation*, because it's okay to use the word *manipulation* just so long as you don't use it in mixed company. If you're in mixed company try to use the phrase "psychological direction," or that sort of thing.

Using presupposition means going in having already manipulated that situation as far as our subconscious mind is concerned. Remember we're now in Core Rapport with our subconscious mind, and we're going into a situation where we know what the result is, we already know that this result is finished, and we're going to act as if the person that we're talking to has already got the stuff that we're going to give them.

We're going into the situation to give them as much as we can, to help them as much as we can. Because when we do that, we presuppose that they're already happy because they got out of the situation what they want. And that means that every pore of your body, every molecule of your body will be acting as if that thing has already happened. You won't have to work to make it happen!

How do we do it? Quite simply, we focus on the end result. Remember what I said before about intent? If the intent is solid, and there's no doubt about the fact that this thing has happened, presupposition automatically kicks in.

How do we use language to presuppose? If we are going to arrange it so that somebody feels absolutely full of gratitude because they've done something good for us, bought us lunch or bought us a drink or something like that, the one thing that they're going to get out of that is our gratitude. So when we go into that situation, say thank you before we've even begun.

Now I know that sounds daft. It sounds stupid. How can you say thank you for something that you haven't got? You can just be full of gratitude. How would you act toward a person that you're full of gratitude for? Well to be frank, I don't know. There's nothing I can give you physically to say, "If you do this, you will look as if you are grateful." No. The easiest way of doing this, as with all of this crap...I almost wrote "shit" there, but I've been told to cut out the profanities...the easiest way of doing this shit is to just do it!

So when I say be grateful, I mean be grateful! Be grateful as if that person has already done the thing you want. If you're in a situation of presupposition, they will follow you. It's what we call social reciprocation. Whatever you do, they will do because you're in rapport.

I'll teach you how to strengthen that rapport in just a little bit, but if you're in Core Rapport, you know that person, and that person already knows you and you know you.

You know that sort of situation where you've been talking to someone for five minutes and they say, "You know I feel like I've known you my whole life!" That's Core Rapport.

That's what you're going to have with ninety percent of the people you get into relationships with and that you get into business with. And that will spill over to the people you connect with everywhere. You will stop even noticing after a while – and this is happening to me now – after a while you stop even noticing people that you're not in Core Rapport with. It's like they just stop existing.

# Games and Experiments:

You know when I talk to people and I say they really should make a game of it, they say "Oh I can't make a game of this, it's too serious. This is life-changing, it's serious, it should be serious, it shouldn't be a game. It shouldn't be fun."

Well, everything I do has to fit three criteria. Number one, it has to be easy. Your subconscious mind is a bright nine-year-old child. It has to be easy. And the one thing a bright nine-year-old child won't do is work. That knocks you right out of Core Rapport. If you're trying to get your subconscious mind to work for you, it knocks it out of rapport.

Number two, it has to be *fun*. **Your head has to be full of dopamine.** I have said this before. You may have heard me say this before. And I can't say it enough. If your head is full of dopamine, you learn better and you retain more knowledge. You're enjoying yourself, and if you're enjoying yourself you work better as a human being.

Simple as that. People say you've got to be passionate about something. And by passion we mean enjoyment. You've got to be having a whale of a time.

And thirdly, it has to be effective. It has to work. But it has to work for both parties in this case. It has to give something to both parties.

Now the thing with games, when we're playing games we're not talking about competitive sports. We're talking about playing the game just to play – just to enjoy it.

We're talking about pastimes, we're talking about riding on jet skis and motorbikes and going for a drive across the desert or just going and knowing that we're giving ourselves a thousand dollar limit in a casino in Las Vegas or Monaco and saying, "Right, we're just throwing that away tonight. We're just going out to enjoy ourselves. If we win we win, if we lose we lose. Who gives a damn?"

So, we're getting to the point where we make everything a game.

Or we make it an experiment! Now the thing with experiments is that there may be a conclusion that we presupposed is going to happen and we're going to see whether that happens or not. Then it becomes interesting and experimental.

When we're using influence and persuasion skills on a game level or an experimental level, two things come into place. Two things now cannot occur as they can with most covert and conversation hypnosis stuff and underground or underhanded or backhanded ways of manipulating people. Two things cannot occur:

One, you can't get caught because you're not hiding any-thing. You're just playing a game. And if someone says, "Hey, are you playing a game with me?" you say, well yeah. And they laugh because it's funny and it's fun.

And number two, if it's an experiment, if they say, "What are you doing?" And they really are pissed. You just wipe that off and think that this particular experiment was a failure. You know that you're going to get the result sooner or later, but that particular experiment didn't work.

This is important because if you see this as a failure then you may never do it again and then you blame the system. As an experiment you can not fail because the result is just a result. Whatever it is.

You haven't been caught because you're not doing anything underhanded. I've seen lots of people trying to do certain things to bring people around to a different way of thinking or to bring people around to their way of thinking, and their success rate – I've watched them and observed them – and their success rate is a lot lower than they claim it is.

And you don't want a lower success rate here. You want to be up in the high eighty or ninety percent. And the easiest way to do that is to put yourself mentally into a situation where you presuppose that you will get the result and then you just enjoy the process and you make it a game to enjoy or an experiment to observe.

You're enjoying yourself. I can't stress enough that people like to be around people who are passionate about what they are doing and who are enjoying themselves! People love to be around those people. It's that shared energy thing. Share yours and you are truly influential.

# Giving People Stuff

This isn't in the actual recording but here's a story from one of the students from the original event. For professional reasons and the delicacy of some of his clients positions we can't say who or what he is. Let's say he's a partner in a very prestigious world wide business.

\* \* \* \* \* \* \* \* \* \* \* \* \* \* \* \* \* \* \* \* \* \* \* \* \* \* \* \* \* \* \* \* \* \* \* \* \* \* \* \* \* \* \* \* \* \* \* \*

"I was running my monthly meeting with my staff from the offices I have in several locations all over the world... and decided to play and experiment with the most subdued of my management staff. This guy hardly ever joins in at these meetings and was on the verge of finding himself a new job.

First I used the Parrot Rapport. After five minutes the guy was leaning forward, smiling, talking animatedly and actually becoming passionate about his monthly report. It was almost fucking scary.

So then for no reason I gave him a pen in mid sentence. He looked at it for a second and carried on talking. When he stopped he put the pen down. Until the next time he wanted to come into the conversation then bugger me if he didn't lift the pen up and hold it the whole time he was talking.

The funniest thing was that at the end of the meeting one of my other managers who's been with me longer went over to the first guy and took the bloody pen off him and put it in his pocket. It was just a biro for fuck sake!

Tell you what though, within a week the first guy had got me twice as many contracts to close in a week as he'd got the whole previous month. Good experiment."

\*\*\*\*\*\*\*\*\*\*\*\*\*\*\*\*\*\*\*\*\*\*\*\*\*\*\*\*\*\*\*\*\*\*\*\*\*\*\*\*\*\*\*\*\*\*\*\*\*\*

The whole point of all these things, making it a game, making it an experiment, working smart not hard – the whole point of this installation, as I said before, is to make friends, not enemies. Because if you do something shallow or something that doesn't give somebody something of value, and then a couple years later their thinking they didn't really like you all that much, then you've actually made an enemy rather than a friend. If people ask about you, your "enemy" is going to tell them all the worst things about you. You want a friend so that even fifteen or twenty years later they recommend you!

I've had this happen to me where people I've worked with who have walked up to me fifteen or twenty years later and thanked me and asked for my number so they could give it to someone they know. I've had that happen to me a lot of the time because of this friend idea. Plus I am a fairly good manipulator. Most disabled people can get that way because we need to. We need to be able to get people to come in with us on things, and that's one of the reasons I'm so good at this.

Giving people stuff is one of the most important things you can do because one of the things people don't do when you give them something is say no. Most people don't look a gift horse in the mouth. They really don't. They say, "Thank you very much" and they take it.

Giving people stuff is a game I like to play. This is just a light thing, but I do want you to try this because it's very, very important. I want you guys to play with this because it's a game, and it gets you started on realizing just what you can do with peoples' subconscious minds and their presupposed patterning and your presupposition that this is going to work. But it is a little bit of an experiment as well, because you don't know how far it's going to go.

The game works like this: while you're having your conversation with somebody, for no reason at all, take something in your hand and hold it for two or three seconds, look at it, weigh it up, carry on with the conversation, and while they are talking away, hand the thing to them. Nod at them, and then give them the thing. They will hold it – it doesn't matter what it is!

Looking down at my desk as I'm writing this, it could be a cup, it could be a mug, it could be my iPhone, it could be a mouse, or it could even be the keyboard. I once made a film for the Internet about this where I did this exact thing with Jane you'll find it on the SvengaliSystemAlliance.com membership pages or on YouTube. It's called the Persuasion and Influence learn How to play the "Hold'em" game.

In the film I call Jane over and just give her stuff to hold. I waffle something about setting up filming something and then hand her first a book, then my iPhone, then my Mac Keyboard and top it off with my glasses before I break down and start laughing - it's a game!

She didn't know I was going to do it and it does really work. You'd be surprised at just how many things you can give somebody before they turn around and ask you what the hell's going on!

Why do you want to do this? Because it's going to train your subconscious mind, and it's going to train other peoples' subconscious minds that this is what you are actually doing – that you are actually giving people stuff and they are ACCEPTING. When you are moving toward a shared goal, and if that shared goal is for both of you to feel good, which hopefully that's what you're going in to do, if you are moving toward a shared goal, they will accept gifts off of you.

If they accept gifts from you, they have to give something back, it's human nature. So when you turn around and say that it's just a little game you play and you get people to hold stuff, they'll laugh and they won't give you any hassle about it at all. And now you've become fun in their subconscious mind. It's a great little ice-breaker as well.

I've never seen anyone get angry with this. It's just a little game that you're playing with their subconscious mind and they won't even realize that what you're actually doing is teaching their subconscious mind to take stuff off you, to receive what you are giving them.

Okay, so you've given them physical stuff. To the subconscious mind there is absolutely no difference between physical stuff or emotional stuff. In fact, to the subconscious mind they are exactly the same. So if you give them something, they will accept that, and they've learned to accept stuff off you. They've learned to trust you because the stuff that you've given them hasn't done them any harm, and it's just a game. It's just a silly little game that you can both play.

Teach it to them and they won't know that every time they do it with someone else successfully that they are running their pattern for *you* and strengthening their trust in *you*.

So remember: all you've got to do with this game is just give them stuff. Anything that comes to hand. I want you to try this over the next few days. I want you to do your Core Profile on your average target person. I want you to sort of step away and observe yourself a little bit because you'll notice that you're being drawn toward people. Go there, see what happens. It's a game. It's an experiment.

Don't immediately go out starting to give people stuff, randomly and say, "that's because I want you to buy a house off me." It doesn't work like that. Not yet. We haven't got to that point.

I will be talking about how to create stuff. What I want you to do in this section, for the next couple of days (at least for a couple days if not longer) is just experiment with this so you're making friends, not enemies. You're getting your presupposition right, you're saying, "Right, you're holding six things," you're getting the client's social relation and family in Core Rapport with you, you're beginning to understand them, you're beginning to work smart not hard, and you're playing and conducting experiments – not doing covert nasty stuff that you might get caught for. Then you become friends, not enemies with people.

Give yourself a break for a couple of days and let this stuff sink in.

## Observation:

I want to tell you a bit about observation. Observation is your most important tool. Watching people, seeing where their hypnotic moments come in. Now, what's a hypnotic moment? I'll tell you what a hypnotic moment is. It's when the subconscious becomes dominant.

Later I'll tell you about how to create this situation, but it's watching for when the subconscious mind becomes dominant, where emotion takes over. And that's all we're looking for. We're not looking for a trance state. We're not looking for anything particularly "Svengali-ish" (it should be obvious to you by now that I just used that name to attract people), but we're not looking for that Svengali-ish approach, but rather the point at which people become hyper-emotional about stuff.

And remember, we've been talking about playing games, having fun, getting people emotional! What you're observing in people and what you need to observe in people is the point where they become passionate, the points where they become wistful…even sadness is a point of subconscious dominance.

I'm going to be moving you toward that. All I'm doing now is planting the seed to observe, to watch people more than you ever did before. And after this you will find that it's almost impossible not to do that.

# Parrot Rapport and the Big Question Mark ?

I'm going to now talk about "parrot rapport" and the big question mark.

I've had a lot of people say to me who've done the NLP thing that I'm supposed to say, "Where would you like to be right now at this moment in time?"

And the person says, "Oh, I'd like to be in the middle of the London Bridge," and I'm supposed to say to that person, "And how would that feel? And what would that do for you? And how would you handle that?'"

You've got to think of all these bloody questions to ask them in order to move them into a situation where they start to feel happy and everything like that. One wonders what happens in the situations where you say, "Where do you want to be right now?"

And they say, "The London Bridge."

You ask, "Why would you want to be there."

And they reply, "I'm jumping!"

"Right, okay, and how would you feel about that?"

"Wet!"

As you can see, you might not get the result you want! You want people to reciprocate in a nice social way, so I'm going to give you another thing that I want you to practice. How to use this in a manipulative way, in a controlling way, in a directing way – a *directing* way – that's better! This is just a thing I started using a long time ago and I use it whenever I want to raise an instant connection with somebody, to become instantly connected to somebody and be seen as being really empathetic and being in empathy with someone. And that's what rapport really is – being in empathy with somebody. It doesn't necessarily mean being friends it just means being the same as. (But your Core rapport does mean being friends.)

How do we do this? You parrot. You build what I call "Parrot Rapport". And you do this using the "Big Question Mark." This is so easy it's incredible. It's an old sales thing that not many people know about, and a lot of people that have come across it and use it well, can manipulate people to the point where that person will virtually give you anything you ask for.

I prefer to use it just to build rapport. It's simple. It's easy. Everything I do is simple and easy, and you will practice, you will start using it, and you will find yourself using it all the time.

One thing that you can do to be in rapport with somebody is to mirror and match them. I know, I know, I know – you feel stupid mirroring somebody. You're not sure if you should put your hand exactly up onto your cheek because they've got theirs that way or if you should just put it on your shoulder and let it sit in more or less the same position or just do exactly what they're doing and say exactly what they're saying, and it just becomes complicated and complex.

The problem with all this stuff, all these manipulation tools that you have to do, is that it's not installed in your subconscious mind. You're not just doing this shit, and you're not just getting on with it, and they will notice that you are thinking.

When you are thinking about stuff you become suspicious, and when you become suspicious, any hope of rapport – even if you've built your Core Rapport – everything just goes out the window because most people will know that you're doing something deliberately. Don't!

At first you will be doing this almost deliberately, but I promise you that you will find yourself doing it, you will discover yourself doing it more than you're deliberately setting out to do it. And if you're already doing this as a salesperson, then stop thinking about it and just do it naturally. Just do it easily. It'll come. Don't worry about it. I promise you.

Parrot – what does a parrot do? A parrot repeats what you say, right? No. A parrot repeats the last thing it hears two or three times. It's a little bit like the old Copy-Cat echo machines we used to have way, way back in the days of the band, and there used to be a continuous tape in a circle that went round a record head and a playback head that was set about three inches apart.

That's how we used to do echo in those days. What would happen is that you would say, "Hello," and it would record, and it would take half a second for it to get around to the play head and you would go, "Hello, hello," and if you do say anything else or if you set the tape to go really quickly, it would go, "Hello, hello, hello, hello…" And it would just echo back at you. That's what parrots do.

If you say to a parrot, "Come on now pretty boy. Who's a pretty boy then, who's a pretty boy then?" It will not say, "Come on now pretty boy. Who's a pretty boy then, who's a pretty boy then?" It will just say, "Who's a pretty boy…"

This is the first thing, step one: parrot. Whatever they say or whatever they're talking about, parrot the last two or three words. They are going to notice this and everyone will notice this – UNLESS you add the magic big question mark!

As soon as you add the big question mark, you are creating something that everybody wants: you are making them interesting. You are asking for confirmation of what they've just said. They can't not confirm it because they just said it!

Some interesting things happen here. For instance I was once talking to Jane and she was telling me about when she was in Italy and she was climbing up the mountainside and I think she said, "and the sun was beating down," and I said, "And the sun was beating down?" And she went, "Yeah."

And every last couple or three words she said, I just repeated them and added a question mark to them. I just lifted my voice and just gave them back to her as a question, and she didn't question this herself, because obviously she must be being interesting. I must be being interested! She, therefore, feels important.

This isn't rocket science, you know. When somebody feels important, when you've made them feel important, they are predisposed to give you more stuff. And remember, we want them to give you stuff. We want their subconscious mind not only to be prepared to take stuff off you, but to give you stuff as well. Then, when we eventually get to a sales situation, it's not even a sales situation!

By parroting the last few words and adding the big question mark you get them to go into their story in much more detail. And notice I say "their story." When they're talking to you about the things they like and the things they're passionate about, the things that their wistful about, "Oh it would be nice to be back there again," as soon as you do that, then the emotion springs forward and they create a subconscious situation, and when people create a subconscious situation they are open to suggestion.

One of the later things we'll be talking about naturally is suggestions and how to formulate them and put them in together. And get really excited about that because that's really good. But at the moment I just want you to experiment with trying this and see what happens. Observe. For the next couple of days, do your Core Profile with the typical target person, notice how the people that you are drawn toward are hitting that target. And remember, you're always going to get fringe players. You're always going to get players who kind of come on to the park only a little bit.

You're always going to get the fringe players and the outside people, but the *core* of the people you are attracted to and the people you are attracting and the people you're doing business with will be in that core with your typical average target person. (And I'm saying "target person" because I don't know whether you're going after a client, a social relation, or your family.)

Parrot rapport, adding the big question mark, observing when they get passionate, and observing that you also get closer to that person, that person will feel closer to you. You will create that person where that person feels that they have known you forever. And I'll tell you why that's happening. Because they are having a conversation with themselves! And because they are having a conversation with themselves, of course they're talking to somebody they've known their whole life. Once they make that association with you, then the next step is very simply and fairly easy.

I have never, ever, ever had anybody suspect anything when I've turned around and asked them questions about themselves. I try this out all the time, and one of the best ones is when I'm in a store and I go to the checkout, I usually make a comment like, "Don't look so happy." That makes them smile. "Don't look so happy. It'll soon be over!"

(They'll start talking about themselves.)

"Yes. I'm not full time."

"Not full time?"

Then they'll say, "No, I work from ten to four."

And you'll say, "You work ten to four?"

"Yeah."

"So it's not full time then?"

"No, it's not full time." And I've just repeated what they said before. It's very simple and it's very easy to have these types of conversations. They will take over the conversation within three or four things and they'll start talking about other things. For them emotional things.

You will not believe the things people will tell you! I tried this out one weekend when we were at Living Coasts in Torquay on the English Riviera. It's a place where they breed protected and endangered marine species, and they're breeding penguins at the moment, and then they repatriate them and that sort of thing. It's a beautiful place and it's really well run.

It's wonderful to go through it, even on a wheelchair, because the animals are not caged as such. Certainly the seals are but the penguins actually wander about their enclosure and you walk through their enclosure! You go through their enclosure so you're in their world, rather than being separated from them. If you've got kids, take them there — and no I am not an affiliate! (Though I wish I was.)

Anyway, there were some people and we were watching the seals being fed, and a woman made a comment, and then I made another comment (which I always do – I talk to strangers incessantly. I mean you can't shut me up!) and so I thought I might as well test the parrot stuff since I was going to be writing about it.

That woman was a complete and absolute stranger to me. Within ten minutes I knew that she was down for a wedding, that the wedding had been conducted at the Paignton Registry Office and then they'd all gone on the Ferry across TorBay to Brixham and they'd had the wedding reception actually on the ferry as they'd hired that, and the bride was wearing pink flowers on a white dress, I knew the family names…she gave me all the information I could possibly use to make so much sense to her being a friend.

I could have manipulated that in any way I wanted. That was only using parrot rapport and the big question mark and that took three questions before I just shut up and listened. And that woman got passionate, she got wistful, she got happy. She walked away, and as she walked away she turned around and said one of the most important things that you're looking for from a customer, a client, a social relation, your family, or anything.

She turned around and although all I'd done was listen, she turned around, looked at me and smiled and said, "Thank you." And then she walked away. That's how powerful this stuff is. I do this three times and I've got a thank you. It would have only been a little shift to turn that thank you into a token of appreciation that I could have gone on to give to somebody else, such as cash.

**All I need to do is to provide something they want or tell them about something I want them to do as if it's already happened!**

# CLASS 2

## ACTION SECTION

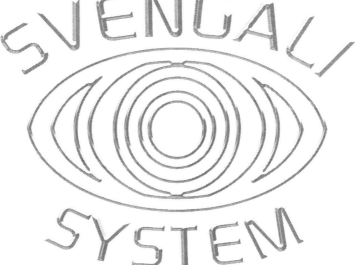

Observe - Listen and observe
the person's subconscious

# Observation

The next step in the Svengali System deals with observation. Now that you have identified your core self through your Core Rapport, it is time to observe other people. Making these observations is the first step towards making it easy to influence them in the near future.

One important point to remember is that when you encounter the right people, you shouldn't have to *sell* yourself to them. The process in the Action Chapter should assist you in becoming more attractive and, as a result, naturally attract other people.

Run a Core Rapport on your typical client.

Once you do this, these clients will be extremely easy to find. As you will see in the exercise below, running a core rapport on other people is a bit different than running one on yourself.

Developing a profile of other people will assist you to quickly understand who they are and what they want.

You can also use this process on your friends, people you want to date, friends, work associates etc.

## Exercise:

### *Create a Core Rapport on Another Person*

Choose a person you are going to focus on. Start with your perfect client.

Figure out what this person does. Ask yourself the following questions:

- What is this person's name and age?

- What is this person's core philosophy? How does he or she view life?

- What does he or she do socially?

- What books and websites does he or she read?

- What tv shows and types of radio does he or she like?

- What is the main problem in this person's life?

- What is the potential solution to this problem?

- Where would you potentially find this person online or in public?

Feel free to come up with additional questions to add to this list...

## The Importance of Identifying your Key Client

Once you understand this person, he or she will become very easy to find.

Perform this Core Rapport process to envision your perfect client. Once you have identified this client, you can then focus on figuring out where to find and meet this type of person. Then all you need to do is go hang out at this spot.

By doing the core rapport process on others, you have just made your work easy and effective because not only do you know who you are looking at influencing, you know where to find them!

Identifying the core rapport on other people is effective for:

—Marketing

—Networking

—Social Strategy

...and more!

When seeking new clients, friends, relationships, this process is a crucial element. As we discussed in Class 1 of the Svengali System when we dealt with Intent, we want to get in touch with your core client and establish a rapport.

**Are your Clients Your Best Friends?**

A new economy means a new approach. The business buzz at the moment is the Client Relationship. The best way to do this is to have your clients be people who you like and would seek out friendships with.

Here is why this sort of friendship is important:

—If your client is someone you like, it is easy to be in rapport.

—People who you have much in common with will be comfortable in your presence.

—You will have a level of understanding with the other person.

—These are clients who will want to come back to you in the future

—Your clients who are your friends will recommend you to their friends and associates. That is an added bonus for you!

At this point, it will be much easier for you and your client to be in rapport. This level of understanding is a large part of what the core rapport is about.

What if you are dealing with Clients outside of the Core Rapport Profile?

There will be some fringe players who are on the outside of your core rapport that will come to you. Perhaps they fit just 8 out of the 10 main criteria you have developed for your perfect client maybe as few as 3 or 4. That is ok. There will always be some people who are attracted to you that don't perfectly fit into your core rapport profile. However, chances are you will be able to influence them to become one of those people!

## Games and Experiments

Ok, so now you have your own core rapport, and also the core rapport of the person you are looking to influence. Great job!

The next step is to work on how we will actually use our powers of observation to figure out how to manipulate them.

## Presupposition

One tip that will help you is to visualize the end results of the situations you want to achieve. This activity is called presupposition.

### *How Presupposition Works:*

1. Visualize the end result you desire.

2. Go into a situation in your imagination planning what you will be doing in advance.

3. Go out and act as though what you have planned has already occurred.

Presupposition is an extremely useful tool to have at your disposal when you want to influence the end result. Use language as a tool along with presupposition. You can go into a situation saying thank you, or whatever else you want to say, before you have even begun. You can just act as though the person has already got the stuff you will be giving them.

See how this is a more gentle form of manipulation? As far as your subconscious mind is concerned, you have already manipulated the situation before you even interacted with anyone directly.

Remember, just focus on the end result you are seeking.

Why do we use the term games?

Are you wondering why we are using the terms games and experiments? Don't forget, our subconscious is a bright 9-year-old child. This child hates work.

It wants to PLAY!

However, if you present this child with games, he or she will go along with you happily.

For any of these processes to work, they have to be fun. Also your head has to be full of dopamine. In this situation, you learn better. When you are having fun and the 9-year-old child is fully engaged, the work you do will be truly effective.

In fact, when you are working to influence someone, you can even let him or her know it is a game.

Plus, when people see you having fun, they will want to tag along. People like to be around others who are enjoying themselves.

## Watch for Subconscious Moments

As you begin observing other people more carefully, you will begin to watch for their subconscious moments. In fact, you can see when someone's subconscious mind takes over.

This is the point when they become emotional. They may get sad or perhaps passionate. These are the points when you can influence them or implant a suggestion.

These exercises below will help you access other people's subconscious moments.

## Exercise 1:

### *Give People Something*

In the following exercise, you will give someone you are talking to an object while you are talking. This game trains their subconscious mind to accept that gift, and give you something back.

1. Engage in a conversation with someone

2. Hold something casually in your hand while you are talking

3. Wait until the other person starts talking

4. Nod at the other person and hand him or her the object

In this exercise, it doesn't matter what kind of object you pick up. It can be a pen, a saltshaker, or anything else that happens to be around.

## Why is this Exercise important?

—It trains the other person's subconscious mind that you are giving them something.

—People are conditioned not to knock a gift horse in the mouth.

—If you are moving towards a shared goal with that other person, he or she will accept gifts from you.

—Once someone has received something from you, they will be more likely to give something back.

This exercise trains people's mind to take emotional stuff from you as well. This means if you plant a suggestion in another person's mind, he or she will accept it. This person has now learned to trust you. In the end, people only buy from others that they know, like and trust.

## Summary

To Observe

Watch and listen for other people's trance moments and subconscious words.

# CLASS 3

Buckets of Beliefs - Behaviours
Experiences and Memories - Levelling the Play-
ing Field - Telling the Best Stories
Absolute Truths - Momentous Moments of
Subconscious Dominance - Silence,
Confusion or the Pattern Interrupt
Using Emotion - Peripheral Players

# Buckets of Beliefs, Behaviours, Experiences, and Memories:

What is a human being? A human being, and every single person that you meet, and you, and me, and all of us, are animals. We have a reptilian brain, apparently, according to the scientists. (Of course we don't have a reptilian brain because we're mammals, and whatever vestige of reptilian brain that there is in there is just simply what you use to lift your arm or put it down.)

I'm looking at modern-day "us," and modern-day us is basically a bucket of beliefs, behaviours, experiences, and memories. That's all we are. It really levels the playing field when you go into a situation realizing that every single person you meet, no matter what mask they wear, no matter what uniform they wear, no matter who they are, is simply, exactly the same as you.

They're simply a bucket of beliefs, behaviours, experiences, and memories. And you can use that bucket of beliefs, behaviours, experiences, and memories to shift and move them toward where you want them to go, providing that where you want them to go is where you want to be.

Let's get this absolutely straight. What happens is a human being comes on to this planet with no more beliefs, behaviours, experiences, or memories than an amoeba. People say we have instinctual things. Watch a child. Watch a baby. The only instinct a baby has is the ability to focus into its body to the point where if its uncomfortable (and hunger is uncomfortable, being dropped on your head is uncomfortable), and it will then get attention the only way it knows how, and that's by making a lot of noise.

The conscious brain hasn't developed. The conscious brain doesn't really develop until the age of about nine or so, because we need to learn a lot in those first few years and so the conscious brain is more or less kept out of the way.

It's a natural thing. It's more or less kept out of the way as our subconscious mind is gathering all the stuff that we need to carry on with our lives and to build up these buckets of beliefs, behaviours, experiences, and memories.

So why is this important? Because once you understand this you'll understand that everybody has beliefs imposed upon them by other people; everybody has behaviours that are just things to do attached to the emotional states that come from those beliefs; everybody has experiences, which come from the behaviours, which come from the beliefs, which come from other people; and everybody has memories, which are simply hoisted on us by our experiences, which come from our behaviours, which come from our beliefs, which are given to us by other people.

And when you realize that, you start to realize that if beliefs come from other people, you could be one of the people giving that other person a belief!

As a hypnotist, I know that completely and absolutely. I train that in all my classes. The first thing I say in my hypnosis classes is this: "Knowing this stuff comes with a shit load of responsibility."

And I'm going to say this to you readers as well. Knowing this stuff comes with a shit load of responsibility, because you are capable of changing peoples' beliefs. And that fundamentally is what gives us our behaviours, experiences, and memories.

And THAT IS WHAT MAKES US HUMAN!

It doesn't really matter whether you want to do this or not because now that you're in the mode, now that you're tapping that energy (especially if you're already doing it as a hypnotherapist or lawyer or businessman, marketer or even if you're a pickup artist) just by going into a situation the way you are now, you are changing peoples' beliefs.

It is fundamental to the human being. We're the only animal that has a belief system as far as we know. Certainly the evidence is that we are the only one that has a belief system, and the only one whose behaviours are based on those beliefs.

We're absolutely incredible beings because we can behave a certain way based on our beliefs regardless of what the physical world is telling us. If somebody in a burning building believes that wrapping a wet towel around their head is going to save their lives they'll sit there and not do anything and burn to death.

Regardless of what the real world is doing to us or giving us, our experience comes from our beliefs, based on our behaviours, and that gives us our memories.

As I said, this is a great leveller. It is really important to get this in your head so that when you go into a situation, you've got your intent, you know what it is you want to achieve, you focus that intention on the most important person: YOU.

Let's take this into a practical situation. You want a great lunch. You want fabulous service. If you go into that restaurant and you sit down and you look at the maître d', you look at the waiting staff, you think about the chef in the kitchen, and you think about the other diners in the place and you think about the friends you're sitting down to have lunch with, and you think about all those people – if you think about them on different levels, then rapport is going to be very, very difficult.

If you think that the waiter is down there on a lower level, the guests are in the middle with you, and the owner of the restaurant might even be above you – in some cases some people see it that way. The person who sees everybody as below them – and remember, this is your perspective, your belief system – the person who sees everybody as below them tends to talk to everybody as if they are below them, and they're the person who turns around and says, "I never seem to get good service in that place." The main reason for that, of course, is that they treat people terribly. There's no levelling.

On the other hand, if you get your intent that you want to have a fabulous lunch, you want to have fabulous service, you want to have fabulous everything and you go in and you use what I'm going to call "Momentous Moments" of subconscious dominance, and you use the question mark at the end of parrot rapport and you humanize the situation so that you have corresponding beliefs with everybody else, you believe that you are no better or worse than anybody else. And believe me, people don't do this because their belief system has been hoisted upon them by somebody else.

Have a look around the world and see who you think are lesser or greater or less than or greater than. And there is always somebody. If you turn around and think in sympathy, that some-body is less than or worse off than you, then you are running a belief system that just isn't true. Even the starving, even the poor, even the cripples are not less than the able body.

You may say, "Oh no no no no no, I don't think like that!" But you are separating those people out. Stop it! Don't separate those people out. Talk to everybody as if they were exactly the same.

People are people at the end of the day. If you want to get an absolutely brilliant lunch, then here's what I do. I go into a place and I find out the name of the waiter or waitress that's going to serve me, and I use it consistently. I ask them where they are from. If they have a name badge I read it very obviously and ask if their name is .... It makes them think I am interested and that I think it important enough to get it right. I build up a rapport with them very quickly and easily because I know that they are exactly the same as me.

I don't want their belief system thinking that I am greater or lesser than them, because I know that I am going to get the very best service from a friend to a friend, from someone who feels that they are on the same level as me.

That leveller comes simply from realizing that everybody really is a bucket of beliefs, behaviours, experiences, and memories. None of those beliefs – absolutely none of those beliefs – have been given them by choice. All of our beliefs have been hoisted on us by somebody else, by society, by other peoples' beliefs, behaviours, experiences, and memories.

Yes, we can consciously become aware of them and we can override them to a certain degree, but we still, on a *core* level – and remember that this is all about core stuff – this is taking persuasion and influence into the subconscious where it's easier to do. When we take those belief systems right down into that level, and we level everything off, then we know we can have exactly what we want and we know that we can inspire people.

### Levelling the Playing Field:

When you go into a situation I want you to **intend** that not only do you have a fantastic situation, but you give everyone around you a fantastic situation as well. That shouldn't be selfless at all, because if you're not **both** moving toward the same goal, you won't get there.

Without **intent**, if you don't believe in your target, there will be a disparity. And remember what we said about the Core Rapport? There will be a disharmony, and there will be a conflict, and as soon as you get a conflict, you get a war. As soon as you get a war, nobody wins a war. Well, there might be somebody with a few more soldiers standing up, and there might be one with a few more buried in the ground, but you don't want a conflict situation.

You really need to understand this at the deepest level. To believe that every single person in the world is exactly the same regardless of their physical state, regardless of their financial state, regardless of anything. Treat everybody with empathy rather than sympathy.

It's very, very difficult to do this on the peripherals of your typical person, your typical target, your most desired friend, client, or partner. It's very difficult to handle the people who are on the peripherals of those. Fortunately, the more core-based that you become, the less you'll even notice those peripheral people.

Those people will just drift in and move out of your life without you even noticing that they've been there, and more importantly, they'll do it without thinking that they've been rejected by you because that just won't happen. What will happen actually is that they will come into your life and they will move out of your life thinking it was their idea. There won't be any connection.

How do you do this levelling? A couple of simple things.

I've already told you one: everybody possesses something that is vitally important to them, and it's the one thing that makes them feel more important than anybody else. Who hasn't been rankled by being called by a call centre and asked, "Hello, is your name Jon, can I call you Jon please?" Why is that?

**Because the most important thing to anyone is your name.**

It's as simple as that. That levelling action of "call me Jon, call me Eric, call me Sharon" is just wonderful. Try this next time you go into a supermarket. Go up to the till, and while you're putting your stuff there, have a look at their name tag. Talk to them using their name. Only one in three hundred people actually does that, even though the person has their name – their most important thing – on the badge on their chest.

Call them by their name. You will get better service instantly. If you ask how they feel, they will possibly access boredom, they may access all sorts of emotions. When you ask them how they feel, which is the next step, then that stranger is now associating you with caring about their emotional state, and their subconscious mind will come forward. Now you're getting very close, very easily, very quickly, into a situation where you are creating and moving toward what I call a "Momentous Moment."

Names are vitally important. Names are the most important thing that you can use. Simply ask somebody's name if you don't know it or use it if it's there in your face. Don't ask if you can use it because friends don't ask if they can use your name, do they? They just use it!

Just use it politely, and don't impose on them who *you* are unless they ask you your name and in more intimate situations, social and business interactions they will. If it's on a name badge they've already given you permission to use their name because you'll find that the people who don't want you to know their name won't wear a badge or cover it in some way.

Just use that and then ask how they feel. Look at their badge, get their name and say, "Hello Jane. You got much longer to go? How are you? You're good? Yes, great. Fabulous." It's as simple as that.

**Telling the Best Stories:**

I can't even tell you the number of times that people have said to me that they've been taught that getting people into a trance state was all about telling stories, that it's all about metaphors, it's all about creating situations to engage their subconscious, to engage their inner child.

In my experience apart from the odd one or two people who are very good story tellers for most of us this works to change their mental state because the person becomes bored and goes into standby. This is not a very productive state.

The fact is that it is much easier to get them to access the story they are really interested in and the one you don't even have to know - their story. Get them telling their story and by default they'll become subconsciously focused. You can do that simply by asking them how they feel! It's as simple as that.

"How are you today? How are things?" That's it. Now you're showing interest. You don't need to do any storytelling, but story-tellings lead to what I call the Absolute Truths. That's anything they tell you which for them, regardless of observed reality. This is where you make such a deep connection with somebody that they will believe they've known you their whole life. When that happens, these people are going to become super clients. These people are going to become super friends, and these people are going to become super partners.

How do we do this? Who tells the best stories? How do I know the best story to tell? Most marketers and other gurus will tell you to tell the one story that you know best: your own. That's great and fabulous if you are writing a sales letter, and I agree with it absolutely, totally, one hundred percent.

About 2 to 3 percent of the time which is the verifiable success rate of most of these story telling approaches. Bloody abysmal I know but accepted as the standard in marketing.

In fact I put a video on the Internet called Cripples, Cars, Hypnosis, and Handjobs. It's basically about me. It's my story, and it's proven to be very popular. People are sending links to it out to their friends and saying, "Have a look at this" probably because of the final bit – the handjobs. (That's got more to do with titles than it has to do with the story, by the way.)

In that situation, telling your story is great. But if you go out to lunch and try and tell your life story to a waiter or try to tell your life story to a store clerk, they aren't going to want to listen to your life story or any other story. In fact, beginning to tell a story is going to cut you off straightaway.

So who tells the best stories? The thing is, the obvious thing that everybody seems to miss is, if you have a story, guess what? It's just like you have beliefs, behaviours, experiences, and memories. So does everybody else. It's back to levelling the playing field.

Who knows the best stories? That's right – the person you're talking to! Instead of telling them *your* story, ask them for *theirs*.

In social situations people are only interested in one thing: themselves. Generally speaking, this is true of all humanity. Any marketer will tell you to tell your story first. Well, I'm telling you to turn that on its head and **ask** for their story.

Get them to tell you their story, even if you say, "Where are you from? What's that like?" Get them to start telling you their story because they will very easily. After a couple of questions like those, "Where are you from, and what's that like,"

"Oh great. Fabulous."

They are telling you their story.

Now these are personalized questions. In a business situation people would say, "Oh well you can't ask questions like that." Of course you can! A business situation is just a social situation wearing a different hat. You play by exactly the same rules. Remember: you are the one with the intent, and they are not. You're catching them off guard.

Now you must know – certainly those of you who are hypnotists must know — that what you are actually doing is Pattern Interrupting. It's not expected. What they expect you to say is, "Who are you and *what do you do?*" Don't. Ask them instead who they are and *where they are from.* This is a very simple and very easy pattern interrupt. And it gets you to their absolute truth. It's an absolute truth. They can't not answer it.

When they answer you come back with the Parrot and the big question mark and they must say, "Yes." Get them to say yes to you 6 or 7 times and that becomes a habit.

Of course, if you just go out randomly, walk up to people and ask "who are you and where are you from," you are inevitably going to get the answer, "Why? Who wants to know?" That person doesn't fit into your Core Rapport.

But if you walk up to the person who you feel most attracted to in that room, most attracted to *and* most attractive to, then that's a leveller. You've got it in your head that they're a bucket of beliefs, behaviours, experiences, and memories just like you. They have times that they feel that the world should just open up and swallow them, they have times of euphoric joy, they have all the experiences that you have.

Once you've levelled that and you go toward those people, those people are already in resonance with you. Maybe not friends yet, but certainly in resonance. Think of it like magnetic vibrations of two things that are magnetic. When they resonate in the proper way they attract each other and draw together. And you'll feel drawn toward certain people. Go to them. Ask them simple questions.

"Where are you from? What's that like?"

Once they start to tell their story, and when they pause – because this is a normal pattern of speech – fill it with the super question mark to build parrot rapport.

"Oh well, actually, I live in Southampton."

"You live in Southampton?"

"That's right. Yeah."

Now, let's play a little game here. It's a game called silence. What happens in a social situation in a game called silence is that nobody likes them, and they will try every which way to fill them – with anything!

Now if you're doing what you do with couples, groups, or even crowds, the target should still be individualized, like the typical person in a couple, group, or crowd.

Everybody is an individual regardless of how many individuals you have in one place. This is something that I teach in my "Hypnotically Speaking" seminar and public speaking thing that I do and on the stage hypnosis masterclass as well. There are only two people in any situation: the influencee and you. Think about it this way. When you are in a theatre, when you are in a cinema, there's only one person in that place from your point of view and focus. There's you, and whatever or whoever is happening on that stage.

When you're in a business situation there's you and whatever is happening in that conversation you're having with the target person. There might be four or five people in the group but you change your focus every time you bring someone into the conversation or push them out of the conversation.

Once you're in Core Rapport, everybody will be individually targeted as far as they're concerned. Even though you're targeting that one specific individual, they will all believe that they are part of that.

The trick is to speak to an imaginary middle distance person knowing that, unless you are specifically focused on an individual because of the subject, then everyone is presuming you are talking to an individual. Never use group terms such as 'everyone here' or 'all of you'. Just use singular language. "You."

# Momentous Moments of Subconscious Dominance:

Why do I say *momentous moments*?

Your whole being, everything you are, everything you want to be, everything they want to be, has been created in moments. When we are talking about phobias, we're talking about a single moment where an emotional state was so intense that our conscious mind couldn't stop the suggestion of behaviour from taking over and becoming a permanent part of our patterning, associating those memories with that event.

This is a time when the subconscious is dominant and in my book that is when hypnosis occurs.

Let's look at it this way. You could be on an airplane a million times, and then one single little event, which may seem like it's going on for a long time, but it's the initialising point of that event – one single little event like a thunderstorm, and you drop twenty thousand feet and you get very close to the sea and the plane is thrown about all over the place and when you land you think, "That's it – I'm never going on one of those again!"

That's a Momentous Moment. It was a Traumatic Moment. Trauma always comes in moments. The result of that may go on for a long time afterward, but it's that initialising point, that one second of subconscious dominance that takes over where you go from one state to another.

119

\*\*\*\*\*\*\*\*\*\*\*\*\*\*\*\*\*\*\*\*\*\*\*\*\*\*\*\*\*\*\*\*\*\*\*\*\*\*\*\*\*\*\*\*\*\*\*\*\*\*\*

It's important to note that this works both ways. Momentous Moments can also be very pleasing and pleasant. At times of joy or physical intensity we are in exactly the same state mentally, it's just the result is interpreted differently.

These mood or mental state changes don't take a long time to happen either. They happen with a snap of the fingers!

\*\*\*\*\*\*\*\*\*\*\*\*\*\*\*\*\*\*\*\*\*\*\*\*\*\*\*\*\*\*\*\*\*\*\*\*\*\*\*\*\*\*\*\*\*\*\*\*\*\*\*

In hypnosis I teach that you are either hypnotized or you are not. You get to a point where you flip over from one to the other. When you are using a shock induction or you are using a confusion technique that is exactly what you're doing. We're creating a moment of subconscious dominance.

That's when your subconscious mind takes over because it has to. You are asking people for their absolute truths when you are asking people for their stories – and remember you're not doing it out and out – you're not saying, "Oh tell me your story." What you're actually doing is saying, "What's that feel like. What's that like? Oh, that's interesting."

You're leading people to tell you their story and letting them go wherever they want and leading them by asking *them* questions and repeating things and putting a super question mark at the end of it, and pulling them out – all the time pulling them out.

All the time you're getting more and more information out of them. You're not *really* interested in the information, but rather in the fact that they trust you enough to give you that information!

When you're doing that there are moments where the subconscious has to take a step back and just check that everything's okay. What happens when people are telling a story?

When people are thinking what to do next, you hear their pause. This is a momentous moment. This is a subconscious moment when they are accessing their patterns. And while they are accessing their patterns, neither their brain nor their mind is paying attention. Hopefully their subconscious is focused on something good.

When you're getting somebody to tell their story, push them toward the good stuff. The last holiday they had is always a good one. Or just ask them what their best experience has ever been. People are people and we all like going back to our nicest experiences, that's why we remember them. Get their Dopamine flowing. Remember that you're in Core Rapport, and you're looking for people who are going to be telling you the good stuff anyway, not moaning and groaning about things.

As you're moving through this, those momentous moments of subconscious dominance come at moments of reiteration or moments of recall, where they have to think about it, or are just lost in moments of emotion.

There are three things that create momentous moments: confusion, emotion, and silence. Simple, easy to do. Confusion, Emotion, and Silence.

## Silence:

Let's look at the last one first. Silence, I've already mentioned this briefly. Social reciprocation states that if there is silence in the middle of a conversation, somebody will say something to fill it. It doesn't feel good. It feels awkward. It's what we call a pregnant pause. It's before somebody says something momentous, because at that point, people are accessing stuff.

Silence is a wonderful tool to use. And we're not talking about the silence where you're leaning forward smiling happily with your head off to one side and nodding demurely. We're not talking about that sort of silence at all.

We're talking about creating a silence where you look like you're accessing your inner mind. You look as if you're thinking some-thing up. One of two things will happen at that point. Either they go into the same state, which they are likely to do because they are in Core Rapport with you.

If you are in real rapport with people, when you go into a state, they just follow you into it. You don't have to swing a watch or tap three times on the table or do anything like that to get them into this state. They'll just follow your state.

The best thing you can do when you're initialising that silence is to think, "I'm going to go inside...and how does this feel?" If you like, you're calibrating. How do you feel? You're judging how this feels and how the conversation feels.

While you're doing that, at that moment of silence, they will come into that subconscious state with you. Because you're in Core Rapport with yourself, and because I'm installing this – and all you have to do is put this in your receptacle in your special place – what you will find happens is that at just the right time in the middle of that silence, you or they will say exactly the right thing.

If your intent is right, you will say exactly the right thing at exactly the right time. Trust yourself. It's one hundred percent certain.

That's the second thing that will happen if the first doesn't, You go into a much better state to influence by saying the right thing because *your* momentous moment occurs!

Oh yes, it happens to you as well, remember the level playing field.

Those of you who work with people a lot, and certainly those of you who work with them in a therapeutic situation know that you do this instinctively anyway. Or if not, you should. However if your intent isn't focused you just don't hit the spot all the time. And that's when your intent waivers. That's when your rapport waivers. That's when you stop trusting your instinct and when you screw up.

This is even more likely working with fringe players. If you go into a situation where you don't like somebody completely and they don't really like you, you may be able to sell them something by creating a persuasive false rapport, but that rapport is going to be very brittle. You won't be able to do any deep connection like this, and you won't be able to leave lasting things in their subconscious mind.

You're not going to be able to leave lasting beliefs that turn into behaviours, experiences, and memories. And they won't be positive. You've got to do that right.

When you know they are your core profile person, and in groups you are only focusing your intent on those, trust your subconscious to say the right thing at the right time. Don't even bother guarding it. Don't even think, "Well that's a stupid thing to say."

Some people may think from an outside point of view when I'm talking with a client or especially on a course, and probably even in this book, sometimes it seems like I'm talking complete and absolute rubbish. But in reality I know that my subconscious mind is going to come out with the right thing at the right time. Every single time.

And those of you who know me quite well know that this happens all the time. I don't have to think about that anymore. That doesn't mean that I haven't thought about it, I haven't read a book like this one, or haven't had it installed, or haven't decided that's a good thing I want to install that. Now it's something that I don't actually think about. Not in the true, "I'm going to think about that" way. I just stay silent for a second or two and the right stuff comes out.

When they are coming to the end of a sentence, you then have a choice. Do you treat it with silence or do you put the super question mark on? If it's initial, judge how you feel.

When you feel warming to this person, and you feel like you are comfortable in this situation just sitting there and looking at each other, then a perfect silence is all it will take to draw them out or for your subconscious mind to have that couple of seconds to come up with the really, really good stuff.

And remember, I'm teaching your *subconscious* mind here – not your *conscious*. If I wanted to teach your conscious mind then I'd say, "At this point you do this and they fall into a trance." And we all know that doesn't happen, not all the time anyway. (Not unless that's your intent!)

Coming back to silence, do you ask the question or do you just shut the hell up? You judge by how you *feel*. You judge by whether you are warm or cold, do you feel good, do you feel bad, do you feel indifferent?

If you are feeling bad, indifferent, if you are not feeling one hundred percent in tune with the person, or more importantly, you're not feeling one hundred percent in tune with yourself, then the simple easy way of getting around that while your subconscious mind is catching up and while it is coming up with the good stuff to say, is do what I said before: do the parrot rapport with the super question mark at the end of it. Just give the last few words back to them and put a question mark at the end.

## IF IN DOUBT DO WHAT WORKS!

So just repeat the parrot, even if it's for a 'long' time. If they are watching consciously they could notice but, don't worry as this will do one of two things. It could either become slightly annoying, or it could become confusing. From a hypnotic point of view both of these are useable. And we're going to move on for now to confusion.

## Confusion or the Pattern Interrupt:

If a person is a really, really good observer, they may notice it when you throw things back at them and parrot them with the question mark at the end, but most people don't. The vast majority of people won't notice it at all.

I would suggest that you don't do this at a marketing or business seminar where all these people have already done my course or read my book – because of course they'll all notice! But the vast majority of people out there in the world – well, you could look at it as far as the manual is concerned, if there was a manual for all of this, you're on page ninety-seven and they're on page two.

\*\*\*\*\*\*\*\*\*\*\*\*\*\*\*\*\*\*\*\*\*\*\*\*\*\*\*\*\*\*\*\*\*\*\*\*\*\*\*\*\*\*\*\*\*\*

Actually the truth is I've put this in on live events and then done it with the first person who has asked me a question. My intent is for them to answer their own question and ALL I've done is PR and it has yet to fail even though their conscious mind knows the stuff, it doesn't notice it!

\*\*\*\*\*\*\*\*\*\*\*\*\*\*\*\*\*\*\*\*\*\*\*\*\*\*\*\*\*\*\*\*\*\*\*\*\*\*\*\*\*\*\*\*\*\*

They are never going to notice this. They are never going to notice. And if they do notice it they will be slightly confused.

How do we know if they are confused? There are a couple of things to look for, but the most important one is silence. When you get confused you get quiet and you frown and you sort of hold your breath. You interrupt your pattern of behaviour for a second or two.

At that moment, if you give them a suggestion, then that suggestion is most likely going to be accepted and reacted to because they are in that moment of subconscious dominance. They are internalising what the bloody hell is he going on about?

That can be created deliberately as an experiment, but there is absolutely no need to do it deliberately. Remember – I'm getting you to realize that you don't have to do these things deliberately. People already do these things themselves all the time! The easy thing is to watch for it happening as opposed to causing it to happen. Watch for it happening! Then it is natural. You don't need to do anything and they don't have anything to 'catch' you doing.

In any situation, people will do this. In any situation, in any conversation, people will fall silent. In any situation, in any conversation, you can throw them back their own stuff with the super question mark their absolute truth that they've got to agree with because they can't disagree with the questions and just wait.

They've just told you something, you've just asked it back again as a question, and if they say no, they are a liar, and nobody's going to admit that even if their situation is wrong. Even if their situation is that they live in a fantasy world they still have to agree. It's their absolute truth.

And it's the same with the silences, the same with the confusion. They will happen! You don't need to force them to happen. They will happen even in a five-minute conversation.

We don't need to *create* confusion. We know it's going to happen. Even if you are dealing with somebody who's done three million four hundred and ninety six thousand persuasion courses, they will still get to the point where they get confused by the conversation.

They will get to a point where they have to step back and have to go into that momentous moment of subconscious dominance. It's a moment when they are not thinking, and when they are not thinking, that's a moment when their subconscious is open to statements, which is what a suggestion should be.

On one course that I was doing, a guy wanted the company that was flying him out to Indonesia to pay for the flight. It was lunchtime and he was going out to make the telephone call, so I told him to parrot rapport and listen for those moments of confusion, and in those moments of confusion say, "You're paying for the flight."

He did that with this person. He was in rapport with the person, and he was in Core Rapport with the person because he liked this person and this person liked him, and just that one statement was all he made.

The person on the phone said, "Sorry, what did you say?"

The next thing he said was "Who's paying for the flight?

And the response was, "Oh, we're paying for the flight."

And he knew damn fine that they wouldn't normally. It wasn't part of their expenses. But it worked. It worked because he just caught that moment of confusion, and I just told his subconscious mind to wait for it and to do what it needed to. I also taught his subconscious mind to give all suggestions as directly and simply as possible.

And that worked.

Sure, you can use this stuff for all the bad stuff, for all the stuff that you see on TV and in movies, all the 'Svengali' stuff. It will work for that. But I don't want you to just go in looking for superficial situations like, "Okay, you're coming to me, I'm going to stop you smoking, I'm going to charge you a lot of money, now bugger off, I never want to see you again you miserable old git."

I don't want you in that situation. I want you in a situation where people come to you as a friend rather than just a supplier of a service. I want people to come to you as a potential partner and potential part of their life rather than something that's just peripheral.

**Using Emotion:**

The other thing: if you do it too much you will annoy them. Yes you will. Fantastic! Great! One of the things I teach is that fear is great. It's fabulous. If people come to you scared, it doesn't matter whether you're a hypnotist or a marketer selling a product or something else entirely. It really doesn't matter.

At the end of the day people come to you with a situation that is worrying them, and because they're in a situation that is worrying them looking for a solution, they're actually scared. They're suffering with fear, and fear is the most driving emotion we've got. It's a wonderful thing! It's beautiful. It's great.

One thing that I teach is about "awe rapport," which is a way of building a peripheral rapport. By peripheral rapport I'm talking about setting up a situation where you don't want a person who's a part of your life, you don't want that person as a repeat customer, you don't care what that person does providing you get out of it what you want. This is when you could use that situation where you want great service but you're not bothered about any lasting benefits for either you or them. It's a nasty way of using it, but you can do that with awe rapport.

Awe rapport is basically putting yourself in the situation where the person is scared shitless of you. They are terrified of your position, or what you can do for them or to them. Fear is a wonderful moment of subconscious dominance.

As I said, it's the most driving emotion we have. As any therapist will tell you, somebody having panic attacks, people who are having phobias, people who have anxiety states, those are the people that most therapists see, in fact it's all therapists see, that's why I am not a therapist! These clients come simply because they have unproductive, unusable fear in their life.

Being able to access their subconscious mind because it's scared is very simple and very easy to do. That's what happens most of the time when people are going into a hypnotic state. It's what happens in most selling states as well, when most clients are thinking, "Oh shit, I'm going to be spending some money here" and they're scared about doing that.

Annoyance is actually based on fear. It's anger. It's a feeling of being attacked, of your personal area being invaded. That's why you feel annoyed.

Remember the example of using someone's name consistently? Well, some people get annoyed when a call centre uses their name too much and they get annoyed because they aren't in rapport with that person. It's almost like they are being invaded.

But you can still use that! Yes you can. You can use it for direct suggestion in exactly the same way as a moment of confusion. In fact, on a social level we do use that all the time. None of this is unnatural. All of these things happen naturally anyway.

You've got to remember that. All of these things happen naturally anyway. You really don't need to do them consciously. Your subconscious is already programmed to do these things.

All of this happens when we make a contact with another person. Sometimes we may be doing that when our target isn't in the best of moods. However once that contact's made, can you use annoyance? Yes.

I allow people to become annoyed. It doesn't take a whiff of imagination to see how they're accessing their subconscious, they are accessing their emotional state rather than a thinking state, and in a non-thinking state a good, positive, simple, easy to follow psychological direction or suggestion will be followed. Absolutely and completely.

There is no way the subconscious mind won't do that if the suggestion is simple and easy. The subconscious mind is a lazy bastard. It will only do what's easy. It's a bright nine-year-old kid.

Bright nine-year-old children might like to play, but they don't like to work hard at stuff. You make it easy, you make it easy to follow, you make it simple, and they'll come along.

It's not always clear for me what situations we're going to be using because I basically don't see any difference between going to a business networking situation and going to a party. As far as I'm concerned, they're both exactly the same. I'm just going to meet some new people and have a whale of a time! That is always my intent.

So I don't attract nor am I attracted by pissed off people. But on the odd occasion it does happen then I use what is there. I don't work hard!

Now I'm not teaching you this for therapy. Let's make that absolutely clear. I'm talking about networking or social situations and things like that.

As far as therapy is concerned, you can read my book "Don't look in his eyes" to find out that I don't use any of this in therapy. If somebody comes to me I test them to see if they're hypnotizable, I bang them under, and get the job done. I don't do any of this in therapy. It's totally unnecessary because I'm deliberately putting a person into a hypnotic state. I don't have to do anything covert or conversational!

I don't need to spend half an hour building rapport with a client because I already have Awe Rapport. If, however, we were at a networking meeting and it's my intent to get some client friends to come on one of my training courses, that's a different kettle of fish and a different level altogether.

If you're looking for clients, I would just go straight for the awe rapport. Instead of trying to make your clients more comfortable, just go ahead and use that discomfort and fear. But remember what I said in the beginning of the book – if you take these things and you turn them into games and you turn them into experiments and you turn them into play, then you can just try them out and see which way works best for you.

Ultimately, I don't notice the times that I have to work because they aren't in my Core Rapport. Since I've done my Core Rapport things have changed entirely in my life. My marketing has changed, my clients have changed, the way I'm doing and teaching, well installing, things has changed completely and absolutely in a wonderful way because everything's so much easier now. I can look around my group of associates and pick out who will be associates in ten year's time from the ones who are going to be peripheral.

The Pareto rule, also called the 80-20 rule, applies to just about everything. If you think of all the people in your life, twenty percent of those are your closest, dearest personal friends, and eighty percent of them are there peripherally (and if they're a pain in the ass you rather wish they weren't there at all). If you stop paying those eighty percent attention, then all of a sudden they won't be there. And then what you've got is a really close-knit group of people who resonate with you, and who you resonate with.

I apply this to my hypnosis training. Only one in five people are somnambulists and go straight under without you even thinking about it. Using the moments of silence, the somnambulists will just slip into trance. If you catch them at the right moment, if you just shut up and you're listening to your own subconscious, you can tap them on the forehead and say *"sleep"* and they'll just go.

If that's what you want to do with this stuff then use it for that. The thing is if you want to influence people and get them to follow and get your shit then you don't *have* to do trance hypnosis.

Certainly for say telephone or internet marketers, you won't be able to do that, or you won't be able to do it to such a dramatic degree. There are only twenty percent of people who will react that way anyway, you can still make use of all this though, even the annoyance, by getting your intent right and Core Profiling your target people.

If you apply the 80/20% Pareto Principle to it, only about twenty percent of people in your circle of influence really stick around, and the rest drift in and drift out again. So with Core Rapport, and once you've Core Profiled your typical target or typical client, then you'll find that you're just naturally attracted to and attracting that twenty percent!

Instead of putting out a hundred percent approach, you're now putting out a much more effective targeted twenty percent approach, and that other eighty percent will no longer be interested in coming to see you. The twenty percent wedge that you're attracting will come to you, though, because they're being more focused on you.

If you're the only car dealership in the town that sells Ferraris, you know that only twenty percent of the people in that city want to buy the "Big Boys Toys." If you market to that twenty percent and nobody else, you aren't going to have that other eighty percent coming in and kicking the tires and smudging up the windows with their kids drooling all over your brand new Ferraris, and the twenty percent that do come in are going to look at it and know they can have it.

You are targeting specifically, and you have to realize that every situation you go into more or less is a sales situation. You're selling yourself to somebody.

The emotion of fear is our biggest driving point. The fear of loss, the fear of being misunderstood (which we call embarrassment), the fear of giving something away and no longer retaining it (like a secret), the fear of being found out… Fear is the driving emotion behind ninety percent of our emotional states.

But we can use any emotion. We can use joy. Anybody who knows me could tell you that I am a joker. I tell jokes, well make insightful witty observations, all the time. And I love to get people laughing because that's an emotional state and a Momentous Moment. You wouldn't believe how many people I give suggestions to while they're laughing and they don't even notice!

My favourite is, "I'm good!"

That is my skill. That is where I am happiest. All I'm saying is that if a person goes into an emotion, if they go into a state of annoyance, fear, etc., you can make use of it. You don't need to create that. People go into those states, so just watch for them.

However even if annoyance is a usable state, that doesn't mean you have to keep the person in that state. Obviously, if somebody was getting annoyed with me, I would want them not to be annoyed, so I would specifically reach forward, touch them gently somewhere impersonal like the back of the hand or the elbow, and just say, "Don't be annoyed."

I have no idea why people come up with all these inverted and complex suggestions like, "You are beginning to enjoy this more and more," instead of just saying, "Don't be annoyed." We're talking to a bright nine-year-old child when we're talking to the subconscious.

Let's look at the word "don't." There is a misnomer that the subconscious mind can't process a "don't." It's complete and utter crap! It's a bright nine-year-old child. It's wilful, obstinate, playful, selfish, crazy and bloody crafty but, it isn't fucking stupid! Of course it knows what "don't" means!

I have hypnotized tens of thousands of people, and one of the first things I do on stage is say, "There's a white line across the front of the stage, and you will NOT go over that white line unless the hypnotist specifically tells you to. DON'T go over the white line."

I have just mentally created a brick wall. I have seen people run against that white line and that invisible wall and bounce back! Don't tell me that the subconscious mind can't process the word *don't*. Of course it can. That's my personal experience, and I am a *very* experienced person.

We are taught constantly by people who have been taught themselves to make these things clever, to make things sound good and who have never truly experimented with the stuff they teach. Shame that.

If you tell the subconscious mind when it's not enjoying itself that the thing it's doing is enjoyable, what are you creating? Number one you are creating conflict, because the conscious mind and the subconscious mind will say, "No it's bloody not!"

That worries me because you are also associating feeling good with an annoyance and not recognizing their state. When you're in rapport with somebody, you recognize their state, don't you? Just turn around and smile and say, "Don't be annoyed."

If the subconscious mind accepts that it can only do one thing with it: change the way it feels, and pick something else. It can't be angry, it can't be annoyed, it can't be scared, so it will pick something else and it will start to feel good.

I've seen it happen time and time again. Actually, Jane does it with me when I'm getting annoyed. She'll put in a pattern interrupt. She doesn't know she's doing it – it's subconscious. And she'll just say, "**Don't** be like that."

You have to change because it's a direct suggestion to the subconscious mind and that's what the subconscious mind does. It creates reality from suggestions. That's its job! Its job is to build up beliefs and behaviours so you get experiences and memories. If you give it a strong enough belief, and you give it at the right time, it will react to that.

That's how you would use emotions. I would not deliberately create annoyance, but I know that people do get annoyed by all sorts of things.

People could be annoyed because you're wearing the wrong colour. People could get annoyed because your accent bothers them. People can be annoyed because you say "fuck" in the wrong place or the right place when you are using it as a pattern interrupt. People could be annoyed simply because they wake up that way!

Not everybody chooses their mood. Even though I try to, I don't choose my mood all the time. It's not always easy. If I want to be in a good mood before working on the computer though, my favourite thing is to just go on Youtube and watch something funny because that always cheers me up.

Use annoyance if you want to, but if you're in Core Rapport, you won't need to very often.

However by getting them to open up you will always use Emotion.

# Peripheral Players:

You will always attract people who are not your core target, these are the ones for whom it feels like you have to 'work' to keep them. You are constantly working at repairing or even recreating rapport.

The rapport should have already happened because you've done the Core Rapport, but you're using the peoples' absolute truth as a way to cement that rapport into place and build friendships. You're not just creating something that isn't there – you're bedrocking in, what is there.

Peripheral players – and I like to call them peripheral players because I see life as a big game. It's a fairly serious game at times, and let's face it, if you lose, that means you won't be playing it anymore.

If you see it in that way, as something to be experienced rather than a problem to be solved, then you have people who are playing the same game as you (your inner twenty percent) and then you have the peripheral players (20% of the other eighty percent who are not quite your core profiled elite).

The peripheral players come over to your part of the pitch and kick the ball around a bit and wander off again. You're not really focused on them anyway, because you're focused on the core, and the Core Rapport has already happened.

If those peripheral players come in and they have something you want to transact, you can let them come in for just a while, sell them something, dust them off, and then let them go away again, but ultimately that's not what you want to do. Ultimately you want to be in a park where everybody's playing the same game.

If you like, you want to be in a park where everybody – and I mean everybody (including the players) – is supporting the same team. Look at the people with the sort of stuff we consider to designate their success. What you will find with the ones who are happy and contented is that they are surrounded by people who are playing the same game, they are all enjoying themselves, they are all going in the same direction, it's great, and they get stuff done.

And then you get the sort of player who might have the trappings of success but is really unhappy. I've met several millionaires in my lifetime who had less than fantastic private lives and emotional lives. And that's because they take that habit of playing the peripheral field in their business into their private lives.

They don't get into Core Rapport with themselves. They don't know who they are or where they are going, and when they're doing their influence and persuasion or have rapport, they're doing it with people who will come in for a little bit and then go out of their lives and never come back again.

If the art of persuasion is just about selling somebody who doesn't want a bicycle a bicycle, then that's so simple and easy. Build the belief that they want a bicycle and sell it to them. But you are never going to see that person again, and you are never going to see the three hundred people that person knows, because they're not going to recommend you to anybody. And they'll also be the ones who copy your bicycle and sell it under their own name.

When you get into Core Rapport, then you attract a person who is in Core Rapport with you, and then they refer like-minded people who are also in Core Rapport with you, and then it goes on with a whole network of like-minded people who are all basically in Core Rapport with each other.

But you've got to know that initial person – that ideal client. Then you've only got to sell to one person. You've only got to find one person, and they will bring thousands of others into your life for you.

If you think Variety is the spice of life don't worry. You will get variety, and people who are like chalk and cheese, but they'll still be in Core rapport with you. Most of the variety is skin deep anyway and involves such things as jobs and gender and even the most opposite appearing people share the same lifestyle, ideals, wants and desires. You can still get the core people and still get craploads of variety, so it will never get boring.

You will also find that when you're playing influence as a game and you're experimenting with this stuff, it becomes more and more interesting to *your* subconscious mind. It's a game, and your subconscious mind knows how to play games! It automatically takes you into playing games all the time.

When you're playing games you don't have to think about it, and that's because your subconscious already has these skills. You're just not applying it to the degree you need to get what you want (not yet, anyway).

The main reason for that is that before the Core Rapport you didn't know what you really wanted. Sure you know that you wanted a certain house, a certain car, a certain person, that nice vase…but now that you've got a fundamental perfect thing that you want in your life and the way you want your life to be, your subconscious mind now knows where to take you.

And while you've been reading this I've been using the skills that I've been teaching you. I've been taking you up and down, I've probably made you slightly annoyed, I've made you laugh, I've done all the things I need to do in order to install this stuff in your head. And I know that if I consciously went over it all with a fine-toothed comb, it probably wouldn't make all that much sense, but I also know it works.

# CLASS 3

## ACTION SECTION

Rapport - Parrot the other person exactly

# Rapport

People buy from and do favours for people they know, like and trust. Getting in rapport with people has to do primarily with resonating the same way as they do. At this point, you become almost magnetic.

The established way of doing this is called mirroring. Mirroring is doing everything the same way as the other person.

The only potential problem here is if you try doing *everything*, most people get suspicious of someone sitting or standing the same way as them. You only need to do one thing the same.

So what type of mirroring should you choose?

—Parrot their words and add the "Super Question" mark to the end.

1.  Repeat the last 3 or 4 words the other person says.

2.  Make these words into a question.

This will make the other person say 'Yes' a lot. When we are in agreement with other people, we are also in Rapport with them!

Do this naturally. Make sure that when you parrot the other person it never seems forced or uncomfortable.

# What a Parrot Does

A parrot repeats the last thing it hears. You can say a few sentences to a parrot, and it will repeat just the last few words. So you don't need to feel as though you should repeat everything the other person says or does. It only has to be the last few words.

When you parrot someone, you have made him or her feel important. As a result, he or she is now predisposed to be agreeable. He or she will be ready to be influenced by you.

You also want this person to be prepared to *get* stuff from you. And of course, you want them to be prepared to give you stuff. This parroting technique puts people in the right frame of mind. They will be ready and open to your suggestions.

## Exercise

*Parrot Rapport*

During the next few days, try to parrot someone who is a stranger you happen to meet.

1.  Ask this new person 1 short question.

For example if you are shopping and talking to a cashier, you could ask. "Busy day?"

2. When this person answers your question, repeat the last few parts of their sentence. Engage in this parroting technique with the last few words of this other person's answers.

So, for example, the exchange could go as follows:

You: "Are you having a busy day today?"

Cashier "No, it isn't very busy. Things have been pretty slow."

You "Things have been pretty slow?"

Cashier "Yes"

You will find that after you have asked another person some questions and done the parroting technique, he or she will open up and start revealing all sorts of personal details. They often cannot resist filling you in on vital information.

**At this point they are fully primed to take in any suggestion that you might offer to them!**

## The Importance of Using Names

Names are extremely important. In fact, they are one of the most important tools you can use. Make sure you ask for another person's name and then use it repeatedly.

Names are one of the biggest icebreakers around. Also if you repetitively use someone's name, you will be perfectly primed to be able to influence them.

The use of someone's name is another effective way to build rapport.

## Pattern Interrupts

Another technique you can use is to ask people questions that they are not expecting. Breaking the pattern that they are used to will throw them off track slightly. At this point, you will be a perfect spot to influence the other person.

For example, you could meet someone and ask the following questions:

—What is your name?

—Where are you from?

These two questions cause a pattern interrupt. People are used to being asked "What is your name? What do you do for a living?" When you ask people where they are from instead of what they do, they will be slightly thrown off.

You did not ask them the question they were expecting. Now you are in a position to potentially influence them. This is called a pattern interrupt.

> *"When someone is telling their story push them towards the good stuff"* – Jonathan Chase

If you do this pattern interrupt process with a stranger, you may have a negative reaction. However, if you do this with someone who you already know is in your core rapport, you will have success.

# Momentous Moments of Subconscious Dominance

Momentous moments of subconscious dominance occur at moments of:

—Silence

—Confusion

—Emotion

These are the moments when you can start to get into people's subconscious and implant whatever suggestions you might want.

## Using Silence:

Social reciprocation states that if there is some silence, someone will say something to fill it. No one likes a pregnant pause!

However, silence is a wonderful tool to use. Because it makes someone uncomfortable you can use it to your advantage to get into his or her subconscious.

*Ways you can use Silence*

> *"Remember, the subconscious mind will only do what is easy. It likes to play, not work hard"*
> Jonathan Chase

1.    Keep silent and look as though you are thinking of something.

2.    If you are in rapport with the other person, they will follow you into that state. At this point they will say exactly the right thing. Or you will say the right thing.

3.    At the end of a sentence, you can stay silent. It could be ok to be silent or for your subconscious mind to tell you the perfect thing to say.

Trust your subconscious to say the right thing at the right time to break the silence.

## Using Confusion:

Most people don't notice that you are intentionally being confusing. When they do get confused, they will be silent.

At that moment if you give them a suggestion, they will most likely accept the suggestion deeply. This process can be done quite deliberately and it will give you great results.

## Using Emotion:

This emotion category covers a variety of emotions but a popular one that hypnotists use is annoyance. It is easy to annoy someone.

In actuality, annoyance falls into the category of fear. When someone is annoyed it is really because they are frightened deep down.

Fear is a great emotion to use, because people will often come to you already scared. They may be scared for a wide variety of reasons. At this point, it is easy to access his or her subconscious minds.

# CLASS 4

Elevator Pitch - Social Reciprocation
The Hypnotic Word!

# See the beast in action

This was a very short teleseminar. The whole point of this is to put it into an entirely practical situation so that you get to see the beast in action as it were.

## Elevator Pitch

Most of us have been in a situation where we are at a networking event, a sales situation or meeting a potential customer or client. We typically go into those kinds of situations seeing them as either selling meetings or times to make business contacts.

Most of us have done network meetings of some kind or another, right? And you've probably heard that you need to have a good description for yourself or your services, what we call an "elevator pitch."

For those of you who don't know what an elevator pitch is, it's a marketing term for a few words that explain exactly what you do for people and exactly what your service or product is, and you need to be able to explain all of that in the time it would take an elevator to go between floors.

Maybe that's thirty seconds for the average elevator (unless I'm in it, and then it's forty). And we've been taught that for years and years as a way of breaking the ice or moving someone toward buying something from us.

I'll tell you a little story about elevator pitches. I was at a networking lunch, and each table had a table organizer, who had us all pass out our business cards. Everybody got a pile of pretty little business cards sitting in front of them – the sort of thing you take home, put in the Rolodex – which might as well be ten miles away from me as I never look at it. I don't even dust it!

If you're reading this book you are probably going to find yourself in one of these networking situations. And you should if you've got any sense! It's where you can really start making contacts and where a lot of what you're learning in this book will come into use.

Sure, you can do a Derren Brown thing and talk to a girl in a pub and make her think her yellow car is red. Big deal. Nobody benefits in any way from that, so it's a waste of time. Don't do it.

If you are going to become influential at least play the game so you both win something real.

As you are more likely to be an entrepreneur - my core profile target is - then you'll know the sort of thing I'm talking about. Maybe you are broken into groups of ten sitting at a table for breakfast or lunch. The person in charge of the table then gets everyone to pass out their business cards or worse, a full brochure.

After getting everybody's cards, you get two or three minutes to give your pitch and tell everybody who you are and what you do. At one meeting I went to, the table organizer said we'd go around clockwise, and he pointed to the person on my left and told him to start.

They all went around, they all had their two minutes, and they each gave their little two-minute presentation, most of which were so well rehearsed and put together even they weren't listening to them. And then it came to me.

And me being a bit of an asshole, the first thing I did is a pattern interrupt!

Remember a pattern interrupt is a great way of causing confusion. In other words, instead of turning around and doing what everybody expects you to do you do the opposite or do something different. That causes confusion, and as I said before, that causes a momentous moment of subconscious dominance!

In other words, when somebody's brain gets confused, it gives control over to the subconscious mind because that thinks faster. It doesn't think as accurately or logically, but it thinks faster!

So when it came around to me, I looked at them all, smiled, which I don't think anyone else had done, and asked, "Could you put your hands in the air please?" And every single one of them put their hand in the air, two, much faster than the others.

Then I said, "Put your hand down if you're here to buy something."

Nobody put their hand down.

Then I said, "Put your hand down if you are here to sell your services or to sell something."

They all put their hands down.

So I said, "Thank you very much. Now I'm going to get on with my lunch!"

It was a complete and utter waste of time for me to sit there and tell them who I am or what I do when they don't want to know. They were all there to tell me who *they* were.

Do you get that? They were all totally focused on themselves. As luck had it I was the last to present but just think the poor bloody sod who began wasn't listened to by anyone at all, and the rest only half listened to.

What happened? Three people asked, "So what do you do, Jon?"

Now they're interested! Now I know who is interested and who isn't! Now I know who to target and who to mark as peripheral players. The ones who didn't ask? These people no longer share the world with me. If they have nothing I want and I have nothing they want what on earth would be the point?

The most important thing now though is that because they have asked it, they HAVE TO TAKE INTEREST. And now they are mine because now I know who to influence.

How do we use this in persuasion and influence? Very easily and very simply. You get into a situation where you meet somebody at a networking event or anywhere providing you are where your targeted influencees will be. You go up to them because you can tell that they match your core profiled target. They are your typical client, your typical customer, your typical business partner – they are the person that you can do business with.

How do you know? Because you know what clothing they wear. You know what sort of job they do. You know what games they play. And you probably found out even more because it's down on a little piece of paper or whatever they use at that specific networking event.

You've done your Core Profile for your target, so you know your ideal typical average person, right? Jane and I know our "Adam" so well, we could walk right up to him in the street and I would be right 99.9 percent of the time because it's so precisely established in our minds.

Go to the people who look like your perfect client. Say, "Hello! Who are you?" They are primed to give you their elevator pitch. By saying, "Hello, who are you," the first thing they give you is their name. And names are important as I wrote earlier.

The second thing they will do will be to tell you what they do, and this is the time to use one of the strategies I wrote about earlier: shut the fuck up! Listen to what they say. They will do their elevator pitch.

Pattern interrupt that, by using parrot rapport. They will be slightly confused, because you are verifying every sentence. There should

161

only be one or two if they are doing it to the average script. This is really powerful because they are giving you and then verifying their absolute truths. They are in a state of acceptance, a 'Yes' state.

That's when you do the next step to take you toward one of those momentous moments of subconscious dominance. You bring in the silence. And then you wait.

Then a wonderful thing occurs that some call....

# Social Reciprocation

Social reciprocation works like this: if you have a silence, some-body somewhere will try to fill it. Especially in the middle of a conversation! If you go quiet and silent, they have got to fill it. When they tell you what they do, all you have to do is say, "Oh, really?" And wait.

Wait until they say the magic words (and this works 99.9 percent of the time): they'll turn around and say, "And what do you do?"

And when this happens, do you think you should have an elevator pitch?

No. If you do have one, and you start to give it to them at that point, you're telling them what you do before they are ready to hear it. They could just turn off. You don't just want them wanting to know, you want them desperate to know. You want them to WANT.

I'm going to give you a simple little phrase that you can use with every single person – five little words. Everybody will love this.

What you do is smile, and answer, "I make people like you happy."

What do you think the next question they ask will be, while you're standing there smiling?

Because of the law of what's in it for me they'll have to ask, "How do you do that?"

Well, by this point they've already told you their elevator pitch – and you shut up so you could listen to it, right? That means they've already told you what bits of you they want! Think about it.

I could say, "I train you to influence and persuade people," or "I train you to get rid of your inner conflict, build up a core profile on the people you would most like to be around and who you would like to be around you and use hypnotically based techniques to positively influence people whilst inspiring them to supply you with whatever it is you need when you need it." That would be a pitch, but it closes, it leaves nothing for them to ask.

So I say.

"I'm a Hypnotist! I can show you how to enhance the experience of everyone YOU meet!"

Hypnotist! I know that every covert and conversational hypnosis and NLP course will tell you to never use that word. Absolutely don't go near it with a barge pole, because then they will **know** they are being hypnotized. Rubbish. Most people wouldn't know hypnosis if it came up and hit them across the back of the head with a swinging watch!

# The Hypnotic Word!

Hypnosis - hypnotist - hypnotise - hypnotize - hypnotic - hypnotically - hypnotised - hypnotized - hypnotizable - hypnotisable - hypno .....

I'm going to tell you to use it. Use it indiscriminately. Use it all over the place! If you turn around and say, "Oh, I'm a hypnotist!" you'll see some people going into a hypnotic state almost instantly. More than eighty percent of people will go into that state just on that word! It is the most hypnotic word you've got. *Hypnosis.*

A lot of people say to me, "That's not covert." Yes it is! It's so far out there and in their face they don't believe that you've just said it. They'll look at you and say something like, "Really! Are you going to make me cluck like a chicken?"

I'll frown and answer, "Why do you want to cluck like a chicken? That wouldn't make you happy. What *would* make you happy?"

Do you see what I've done there? Very quickly and easily I've gone from "what can I sell you" to "how can I make you happy?"

Just using a couple of pattern interrupts, not giving them what they were expecting – and if we had interrupted them a couple times during their elevator pitch and parroted back what they said with the question mark at the end like we learned to do earlier, giving it back to them as if we're clarifying what they said to us, as if we're interested in what they've said to us, we are building rapport – and we're building it so fast!

At the end of two minutes that person will feel like they've been talking to you for their whole life. And that's because for those two minutes they've really been talking to themselves who of course they have been talking to for the whole of their lives! And then all of a sudden, you hit them with the magic word: hypnosis.

The problem with covert hypnosis and conversational stuff, that it gets so clever you forget the point of it. The point of it is to get the person on your side. To influence them so they want to give you what you want and feel good about it.

Life isn't a bloody battle and neither is this. It's a **game** sure but it is not a **contest**. If you can get what you need with two or three simple words what more do you get being the Poet-bloody-Laureate except for a good seat at the Queen's official birthday banquet. The thing is just like a football game history will only record the number of goals you score, not the way you scored them.

So what if you aren't a hypnotist? Well, you are doing covert hypnosis and influence and persuasion techniques, so you aren't lying if you tell them that you're a hypnotist or that you have recently been studying a style of hypnosis.

Following that you can say, "I'm an influence and persuasion expert. I influence people." Or, "I install stuff." Use whatever terminology you like, but these are all powerful words or hypnotic phrases. They all communicate the message that *I do something to you*.

Influence, persuasion, install – use the words that are so un-covert, so overt, they totally hide what's happening. As any magician will tell you, the best misdirection is to do what you are doing right under their nose. They won't believe what they have just seen. And more importantly they won't know what it is they are looking for.

What a lot of people forget with hypnosis is that the first 'hypnotist' on record was a guy named Charles La´Fontaine, a Swiss magician. He watched Mesmer doing his stuff and thought, "Oh, if I get people swooning like that when they're on stage it will look really, really good!"

Now the beautiful thing is that everyone in the western world over the age of 5 has a pattern for hypnosis. They already know what that situation should be like. Take them into that situation. Every single person in the world has a pattern for hypnosis and has a pattern to be influenced. The strongest word is hypnosis.

I'll tell you about someone I worked with on the same stage at a showcase years and years ago, so I guess you could call him a colleague. He was a young man who is probably the best magical entertainer I've seen for eons, and his name is Derren Brown.

Derren does a wonderful thing when he goes out on stage with two thousand people. The first thing that comes out of his mouth is, "Nobody will be hypnotized on the stage tonight," and then he gets volunteers to come up for different skits and then bangs them under the whole time they're on stage!

It's only because he knows the people who are likely to come up on stage, and who are likely to volunteer, are his core people. It's the same with you. You know who is likely to get into a conversation with you – they are your typical person, so you are their typical person as well!

Maybe they don't understand this at the surface level, but they understand it at the Core level, and so they find you interesting as well. What happens then is that you're putting them on the back foot by saying, "I'm a hypnotist. I influence people."

And if they say, "Well how do you do that," you can then say that you sell nutritional products (or whatever it is you sell or do).

"How does that influence people?"

"It influences them to get better! How would you like to feel?"

And now you're having a conversation. The whole point of influence and persuasion is to get you into the conversation. It gets you into the conversation so that you make friends with these people.

Think who does you favours. Think of who recommends you or refers people to you. Think of who says, "Oh, I'll do that for you!" Is it your enemies? Do enemies buy from you? No.

So all of this coupled with the presupposition, coupled with the Core Rapport, and everything else here, you are going to get results!

I'm not going to try and wrap this shit up in so much flim-flam that it becomes a trick that only I know how it works. (For those of you who don't understand, "flim'flam" is what magicians call all the words that go around doing a simple little trick and used as a distraction.)

A lot of what people do in networking situations is flim-flam. What I'm doing here is cutting out all of that because it's unnecessary.

What will happen as you start to talk more to people is that they will start to tell you their stories, and as soon as they start to tell you their stories you can stick the question mark at the end of your parroting and you've got them going and you're into a situation where they're having a whale of a time!

As soon as they start to have a whale of a time, as soon as their head starts to fill with dopamine because they feel good, you create an attachment, what's called in nlp circles an anchor. You attach those emotions to yourself, and what you want is for that person to enjoy talking to you. Then the next time you go to that network, that person is going to come up to you and say, "Oh, hello Eric, how are you! Come and meet..."

And before you know it that one contact has become seventy-three. And those seventy-three contacts (or friends, since we call our clients friends, because that's the whole point of all this) become even more.

All charismatic influential people do this. They all make people feel good, and so they make a connection.

Clients will still be your clients, but count them as friends first. You're getting rid of the mask, and when that happens, your Core is talking to their Core, and you're breaking the pattern.

You don't need an elevator pitch anymore because by the time they get to point where they're asking you what you do you can go into so much detail it's amazing. They're actually interested!

If you go into a situation and you say, "Hi, I'm Reg, and what I do is..." you know what they're thinking about? Their elevator pitch. And all they're doing is waiting for you to finish. You do your elevator pitch, and then they do theirs, and nobody's listening to anybody. I see it all the time at networking meetings.

People want to know how they can put all of this stuff into marketing, for example. You put it into marketing because when you've got a typical ideal client, you learn to write a marketing letter specifically for that person.

If you look at my marketing materials since I've done this, you can see that I'm writing a personal letter to "Adam." It might have your name on it, but it's Adam I'm writing to. I know the guy.

I know what he does for a living. I know where he lives. I know who he lives with. I know what clothes he wears and what he's eaten for lunch. I know what TV shows he watches. And because I know my typical client so well, that personal letter *feels* personal to eighty percent of the people who read it.

Will this work a hundred percent of the time? No. I don't think anything does. It will work eighty percent of the time. **I'm aiming at 20%**. Twenty percent is such a small number you won't even notice the failures.

One of my clients when I originally taught this stuff had an amazing situation before I was even finished teaching him. He had been booked to do a big outdoor festival in New Zealand, and it's a huge event. That means all the accommodations get booked solid, and it's very hard to find a place to stay.

He had accepted the booking but hadn't yet asked for any accommodation. Without trying, without thinking about it, just having done the Core Rapport, having a powerful presupposition and intent, and having had the first part of the course installed, he just naturally and organically got what he wanted.

He was in such rapport with the woman handling things, not only did the people who booked him find him a place to stay, but they offered to pay for it as well! He presupposed that this woman was going to be able to "conjure up accommodation out of thin air." He acted as if she had already done that and she did it!

He wasn't consciously doing anything because it was already in its place, in his "ME Receptacle, and subconsciously he set it all up so that he and his partner ended up going to a festival that they were already planning on attending, getting paid to be there, and were getting free accommodation!

For next year's event he's thinking about asking them to pay for travel expenses too.

And aside from the wonderful fact that he got everything he wanted, the added bonus is that the woman who did all of this for him never felt like my client (who is also a friend, remember) had manipulated her – because he hadn't! It had all just happened organically.

He felt great and got what he wanted; she felt great and got what she wanted too. And that's rapport. It's getting people to want the same things that you want, and when that happens, everybody's happy.

**And it just goes in there, with no effort.**

His partner, who had only learned a couple of the things peripherally, also had an experience like this. It just so happened that she needed to get a hair appointment as soon as possible, and she got on the phone to her usual hairdresser, who is quite expensive and very busy, and when she got off the phone she was beaming and exclaimed, "It works!"

My client asked her what she meant, and she explained that without trying, just by having the presupposition and a couple of other little things, she got an appointment for 3:30 the next day.

What's more, is that the woman at the hairdresser's felt like my client's partner had done the hairdresser a favour because they aren't normally able to fill empty appointments at such short notice. She actually thanked my client's partner for taking an appointment at such short notice!

Now, if his partner had done this full course or read the whole book, she would have known to anchor that by saying, "Next time I need an appointment I'll do exactly the same thing for you."

Do you see how I've anchored that? Next time *I* need an appointment. I'll do exactly the same thing *for you*. It comes across like she's doing them a favour by both of them getting what they want. That's a simple little anchor. That woman was in such a good mood because she'd been able to fill a spot that was going to be losing her money. It would have been so easy to anchor that.

We've forgotten that normal good manners make for a bloody good anchoring system! What I suggested my client do when he saw the woman who set up his booking for the festival was to simply say. "Thank you" or send her a bunch of flowers or something else nice, because when you do nice things for people and make them feel good, that anchors the nice feelings to you!

When you do your Core Rapport with your clients, you're no longer dealing with the assholes where you have to work so much harder and they're just going to hate you anyway. That goes out the window. You're only dealing with nice people from now on.

Can you influence complete and utter strangers? Of course you can? Everybody that you've never met is a complete and utter stranger, but some of them will be your enemies no matter what you do, and those people are no longer going to be attracted to you, and you will no longer be attracted to them.

# CLASS 4
## ACTION SECTION

Access their mind - Fire the person's
imagination and emotions

# Access the Mind

We discussed how to spark imagination and emotion. We can trigger pattern changes by directly suggesting that these changes occur.

## The Elevator Pitch

An elevator pitch is a short phrase that explains your aspirations and goals that you could potentially pitch to someone between floors on an elevator. Many people in the old marketing mindset worked feverishly to concoct a pitch so that they could hit people with it quickly.

### Here is the revised elevator pitch

—Listen to what the other person tells you about what they do.

—Wait until they ask, "What do you do?"

—Simply smile and say, "I make people like you happy."

—When they ask how (which they will) state "I am a ------- AND A HYPNOTIST [or I also dabble with hypnosis.]"

"Hypnotist" is in fact the most hypnotic word that you have. When you tell people this fact, 20% of people will instantly go into a hypnotic state.

The point is to get the other person on your side, so he or she will *want* to give you what you want.

## Changing Someone's Emotional State

When you are working with someone and you want to change his or her pattern of thought, it is important to directly suggest it. Speaking directly is an extremely effective tool and will go quickly into the person's subconscious. After all, 9-year-old children can understand and respond to basic commands.

So, for example, what do you do if you are working with someone and seeing that this person is beginning to seem annoyed?

Here is a process that will get this person in a better emotional state:

—Simply put your hand on the person's shoulder or elbow - somewhere appropriate.

—Simply state, "Don't be annoyed."

This quick and easy statement will go directly to this person's subconscious. He or she will take another path with his or her emotions.

# CLASS 5

Repetition - Anchoring - Fascination
K.I.S.S. - Installation - Awe Rapport
Give Don't Sell - The Confidence Trick
The Give Me More Pattern - The Emotional Tools
of Influence - Putting it All Together

# The Five Stage Formula

In this last class I'm going to tie up the five steps to using influence as a formula and those are:

**Number One: *Intent*** – know exactly what it is you want to achieve, remove doubt and focus on the result.

**Two: *Observe*** – watch and listen for their Momentous Moments, for their subconscious hypnotic words.

**Three: *Rapport*** – parrot what they say back to them, don't mirror all their stuff, match what they say exactly, stick a question mark on the end.

**Four: *Access their mind*** – you must access their mind. You access their mind by firing their imagination and their emotion. You trigger pattern changes by suggesting them directly.

**Five:** And most importantly, the fifth step is that you *test*, because if you don't test the result you don't know that it's happened. You test the result and the easiest way to do that is to attempt to trigger the old pattern and see whether it's changed, or trigger the new pattern at will and see if they'll come along with you.

This is a very basic way of looking at the whole thing but you know the experts in anything always use the basic approach. That's why everything an expert does looks so easy - it's because they only do the easy.

# Repetition

Repetition is vital. It's how you learned as a child. You learned to speak words by listening and seeing the words associated with things over and over and over and over again. That's how your subconscious mind works. When we repeat suggestions, we call it compounding (or at least that's what it was called back in the old days). Compounding is making a suggestion and driving that suggestion in until it sticks.

First of all, let's have a look at repetition. Repetition. People are scared to repeat things when they are doing influence or persuasion. And the reason they seem to be scared to repeat stuff is that old thing of getting caught out, but remember, we've already obliterated the getting caught out because you're playing a game!

You're playing a game. You're experimenting, so how can you possibly get caught out? If you do get caught out, explain to them exactly what you're doing. Explain to them *exactly* what you're doing. And they'll go, "Oh, right, okay, how does that work?"

You'll be surprised. I've never yet been caught and had somebody say, "How dare you do that with my head?" It doesn't work like that. People's minds don't work like that. Mostly people will then get even more receptive.

Remember, you're only doing this with your core people. So, even if they do find out what you're doing, and recognize it, it won't stop it working. Repetition. Repetition works.

Back in the early 1900's, there was a guy called Emile Coué who came up with a thing called a Couéism. Basically it's self sugge-tion. No, not self trance, self suggestion. There really is no such thing as self hypnosis. The Couéism however became really fa-mous well after the guy kicked the bucket and became for a short while the in thing around the late sixties. Now everybody has heard this at some point. It's even in a John Lennon song. And that's the phrase, "Every day, in every way, I'm getting better and better."

We know that if you say that to yourself ten times a day when you wake up in the morning, ten times at night when you go to bed at night, you start to feel better. It's repetition. If you think something once it's just a thought. But if you think it seven times it's a habit.

It's the same with suggestion. Give it to them once, it may or may not work, give it to them seven times and it can't *not* work. It's one of the things I'm doing when **I'm installing this stuff into your heads**. I'm repeating stuff. I'm compounding ideas. I'm bringing them back in all the time.

I do that quite naturally. Now I'll do it to the point where it's hard for *me* to actually catch myself doing it. I don't know about you, but most people will say that conversation with me isn't boring even though it might be repetitive, because when I do repeat things I just bring it straight back in and I just shove it in so fast that it just happens. It's natural.

That's the secret of repetition: one, two, three words and if you repeat one, two, or three words, nobody's going to notice that you're repeating that thing. If I want somebody to smile I'll say the word *smile* and I'll put the word *smile* into smiley, smiley sentences and really get them thinking about smiling. There's "smile," "to smile," and there's "smiling" and there's different ways that you can just say that one word over and over and over again and put that word into all sorts of sentences.

The other way of doing that so that it doesn't become boring, so that it doesn't become noticeable is to repeat the word several times in one sentence. You can do this as well with their name. You can repeat their name several times in one sentence.

Derren Brown, in his book, *Tricks of the Mind* recommends that when you're learning somebody's name, you ask them for their name and then you do repeat it seven or eight times in the next couple of sentences. By the time you've done that it will be embedded in your head. These things work – trust me.

\* \* \* \* \* \* \* \* \* \* \* \* \* \* \* \* \* \* \* \* \* \* \* \* \* \* \* \* \* \* \* \* \* \* \* \* \* \* \* \* \* \*

Note: If the conscious mind does notice anyway ignore that. Influence, especially using hypnotic approaches and techniques, is about the subconscious Mind, not the conscious Brain. Personally I don't give a toss what the brain is telling me as I know for sure they will do what the mind believes.

\* \* \* \* \* \* \* \* \* \* \* \* \* \* \* \* \* \* \* \* \* \* \* \* \* \* \* \* \* \* \* \* \* \* \* \* \* \* \* \* \* \*

The Couéism works. The only problem with the Couéism, "Every day, in every way, I'm getting better and better," is that it's too generalized. It's not focused enough.

By the way, there is nothing you are learning in this book that wasn't around eighty to a hundred years ago. There is nothing in NLP that wasn't around two hundred years before NLP. There's nothing in hypnosis that hasn't been around forever. This is all simply a way to put it all together so that it installs into your head so that you are not even going to have to think about this stuff.

In fact, you'll probably find that you'll step outside of yourself when you observe yourself doing it, rather than actually having to go out there and deliberately do it. And of course, if you're thinking about it, then you need to do it more because you need to get it to the point where it just becomes subconscious. Just as I'm installing it now, right now, right this moment in your head.

Have you ever played the game, "My word, you do look ill"? It's a little game we used to play in school. When I was a teenager we'd pick somebody, preferably somebody younger, and then twenty of us would decide to say to that person all day, "Well, what's wrong with you? You look ill, you look terrible, oh dear, you look..."

The chances are that that kid wouldn't come into school the next day. Their mum and dad would call in and say, "I'm sorry but he can't come in. He's sick." Repetitive suggestions work wonderfully well!

# Anchoring

There's a thing in Neurolinguistic Programming that they decided to call Anchoring. Basically, what they noticed was that certain anchors bring forth certain effects, so that there are behaviours associated with beliefs. How they made this startling observation, I've got no idea, but they called it anchoring.

I think "anchoring" is a bit of a silly term for it because basically what it means is setting up an attachment, a behaviour. I think an attachment, or a habit, is just another way basically of saying anchoring. I think calling it an attachment is more descriptive because an anchor holds something in one place, whereas an attachment is something that stays with that thing wherever it goes. And your attachments go with you wherever you go.

Attachments are simple little things. They are not complex, they are not complicated. You do not need to set up complicated anchors. In fact, I'm telling your subconscious mind not to. Go for the simple stuff. Go for the simple anchors. And because NLP has been around for a long time now and because you now know what I am talking about, I'll keep it simple and use the word anchor... or attachments... ;-) [wink]

\*\*\*\*\*\*\*\*\*\*\*\*\*\*\*\*\*\*\*\*\*\*\*\*\*\*\*\*\*\*\*\*\*\*\*\*\*\*\*\*\*\*\*\*\*\*\*\*\*\*

For the record a post hypnotic suggestion - that is a suggestion directed to happen after the hypnosis connection has been terminated by the hypnotist - is also an anchor. Told you it was simple.

**I'll give you an example right now of a simple anchor.**

When we hear a police siren, we subconsciously know that it's the *get out of the way* anchor. When we hear church bells, we think of churches or weddings. And our favourite anchor, as far as bells go, is the sound of a cash register. And certainly in the western world, that has its own connotation: that wonderful word, *ka-ching*!

\*\*\*\*\*\*\*\*\*\*\*\*\*\*\*\*\*\*\*\*\*\*\*\*\*\*\*\*\*\*\*\*\*\*\*\*\*\*\*\*\*\*\*\*\*\*\*\*

How do you set anchors up? When you are observing somebody you notice that they do stuff. They have patterns.

Now, we've all read about eye accessing cues and if somebody looks up and right they're imaging something visual, and if they look down and left they're thinking something up and apparently you can tell whose lying and who's not lying by these.

Personally, I don't think this is true. To catch a liar what you've got to do is watch for patterns that are associated with things that you know are absolutely true and then just watch them break that pattern. It's the whole face. It's the whole way they look. It's the way they pause. (It's another book!) But they do have their own personal anchors. They have their own personal attachments. Watch for their personal attachments, their own patterns.

What are you looking for? Maybe when somebody's talking about something that they're wistful about, some place or time they wish they could return to. Maybe they'll touch the table in a certain way. Maybe they'll touch the back of their neck. Maybe they'll look up in a certain way. These are people's anchors. As soon as you hit an emotion that you want to produce in that person, watch what they do.

Now, I know what you're going to think. You're going to think, "Oh, he's going to get into mirroring here" and that you've got to do exactly the same thing. Yes, absolutely. It's the only time you should use mirroring. But NOT full body. Just the mannerism. What poker players call a 'tell'.

Mirroring is not for building rapport. Mirroring is for firing anchors, in my opinion. Here's a little poker tip: When you're playing poker with somebody, watch for their tells. When they've got a bad hand and they throw it away, watch for that, and then **you** use whatever they do when they throw the hand away to intentionally fire "you've got a bad hand."

People ring me up all the time and say, "Will you hypnotize me Jon, and make me a better poker player?" And my response to that is usually, "It's easier for me to teach you to make everyone else at the table a crap one."

I have a habit: when I'm thinking, I touch my nose. According to all the body language books I've ever read, that's telling everybody that I'm telling lies because I'm trying to hide behind my hand, but that's just not the case. I touch my nose when I'm thinking; that's my anchor for thinking. That's my attached behaviour, my attached pattern for thinking. It's just touching the side of my nose.

Now that you know that, if you and I were talking face to face and you wanted to get me 'thinking' about something, all you'd have to do is touch the side of your nose to fire *my* pattern. I wouldn't even know it was being done, even though I'm telling you about it now.

The beauty of all this stuff, and the beauty of firing patterns, is that nobody will notice you doing it because we're talking about firing an attached pattern, firing a habitual little thing that they do. We're not talking about mirroring them totally like they do in NLP. We're not talking about following their body language in every way possible. We're talking about doing something insignificant that they don't notice that they are doing subconsciously so they won't notice you doing it subconsciously even though you're doing it deliberately.

They won't notice you doing it because they don't know they are doing it themselves!

When I tell you to mirror that one little gesture, I mean mirror them. If they touch the right hand side of their nose with their right hand, you touch the right hand side of your nose with your right hand. Do it exactly the same as they did when you want to fire that emotion.

And remember when you're observing, you're looking for emotional states. Forget the words they're saying, forget the concepts they're putting over. Watch the emotions. Remember, you are dealing with the subconscious child inside. You are not interested in what the conscious mind or mouth is doing.

There are only two mental processes going on at any one time and the subconscious one is the one we're aiming for.

I could say at this point that you've got to do this, that, and the other, but really all you've got to do is think of the person in front of you as a subconscious process, as a bright nine year old child. If you're in a situation where the person is above you, bigger than you, more important than you, by some sort of pecking order, I'll tell you what, just imagining them as a bright nine year old child brings it all down and it's very easy to be in a position where you feel that person is equal!

At the end of the day when you strip away all the things that we are, when you strip away all the things that we have, when you strip away all the things that we do, we all want the same thing: we all want to play! We all want to get to the point where we have enough time where we can play.

You know, if you talk to people about what they are planning for next year, they won't say, "Actually I'm planning to go work in an office nine to five every day for most of the year." They'll turn around and say, "Oh, we're going to Malta next year!" Everybody wants to play.

Remember that you're talking to a bright nine-year-old child. Look for what the nine-year-old child does. All of the important anchors that people fire are developed before the brain kicks in, before touching yourself in a certain way is inappropriate. And you still do it. You still do those things, those childish things. Watch for them.

Listen to what I'm saying to you very carefully. I'm not suggesting that you impose patterns or that you impose anchors. What I am suggesting is you use what's already there; you use *their* stuff. Their subconscious minds will recognize their stuff a lot faster. You don't have to teach it to do something.

# Fascination

\*\*\*\*\*\*\*\*\*\*\*\*\*\*\*\*\*\*\*\*\*\*\*\*\*\*\*\*\*\*\*\*\*\*\*\*\*\*\*\*\*\*\*\*\*\*

Fascination: Hypnotically the word means to capture or attract attention.

That is of course the attention of the subconscious mind. And as we all know the brain can be functioning doing stuff at the same time as the mind being fascinated. Watch a young child walk across the room never taking their eyes off the TV for a second.

I guess in Svengali terms it makes you think of the old swinging watch or pendulum. Happily that still works.

\*\*\*\*\*\*\*\*\*\*\*\*\*\*\*\*\*\*\*\*\*\*\*\*\*\*\*\*\*\*\*\*\*\*\*\*\*\*\*\*\*\*\*\*\*\*

I used to teach a thing that if you wanted to get people doing something, if you wanted to get people into a fascinated state where you could put in a suggestion, you could try tapping rhythmically. You can do this with a fork, you can do it with a knife, you can do it with a finger. Just tap rhythmically until you see them look at your hand.

This is an old trick, I mean this is a really old one, but you can use it. You can use this where you tap rhythmically, keep a beat going, and you tap rhythmically with your index finger on the arm of the chair. You wait until their eyes get drawn to it, get fascinated by it and you give them a quick suggestion.

As I wrote before, they fall into these moments of fascination anyway, and certainly when you're asking questions and putting a question mark on the end of their words. They've got to access more and more complex and complicated situations and you get to the point where they'll drop into that state where you can give them hypnotic commands that we call suggestions, and you can build concepts into their heads by using very simple things. That's one way of getting that fascination.

The other way is firing their emotions – firing the emotions that you want. Most people will go into emotions that they want to be in anyway. How can you steer somebody to get into an emotion that is opposite of what they're in?

**I'll give you an example.**

If you're in a situation where somebody's in a bad mood and you want to get them into a good mood, it seems logical and like a good idea to break the bad mood first, and then gently bring them into the good mood, creating anchors and then creating emotional states so that you can bring them into that state.

But how do you break the bad mood in the first place? I find it very simple, very easy because I do know that there are certain things that break people's bad moods no matter how bad they are. (And remember that I'm talking about my core target.)

Certainly the thing that's easiest for me is this: laughter. Nothing makes me smile more than somebody laughing. It's a pattern, it's an attachment.

How can you break somebody's bad mood? Say, "You're in a bad mood. Go into a good one!"

\*\*\*\*\*\*\*\*\*\*\*\*\*\*\*\*\*\*\*\*\*\*\*\*\*\*\*\*\*\*\*\*\*\*\*\*\*\*\*\*\*\*\*\*\*\*\*\*\*\*\*\*\*\*\*\*\*\*\*\*

I know that seems like it's not covert, that it's not secret. I'm going to get caught out doing that. If they're in a really emotive mood, however, you know their subconscious mind is so much in control their conscious mind will not even notice you said that. It will pattern break them completely!

Certainly their conscious mind is attuned for somebody saying, "Oh, why are you in such a bad mood? Ah, I tell you what, why don't we..."

Nobody's expecting somebody just to walk up to them and say, "You're in a bad mood. Go into a good one!" That pattern break is so awesome. It's one I use on myself. Believe me, when I go to do a marketing thing I have to use it on myself a lot. I say to myself, "You're in a bad mood. Go into a good one." Nothing fancy.

It sounds psychologically inept. I know people think that it's got to be more complex than that, more *complicated* than that, but it doesn't. Remember, we are talking to a bright nine-year-old child!

# K.I.S.S.

There's an old marketing thing and if you haven't come across it you ought to. Imagine this embossed on your forehead. Have it engraved on your glasses. Have it tattooed on your fingers.

It's K.I.S.S. – Keep It Simple Stupid.

Now the end one, whether you want that to mean that you're stupid or whether you should treat everybody as being stupid, it doesn't matter.

By stupid, let's say that's childish. So keep it simple and stupid, illogical. Don't use complex, complicated anchoring patterns. Watch for their simple anchoring patterns. Use what's there. Listen very carefully; use what's there.

Remember, even things like smiles are anchors. So are names and words. Why use stuff when words can work even on my phone. Don't use tapping your finger on a chair when you want somebody to go into a specific state or a specific place of recall, for instance. Don't use tapping on the phone because you sound like an idiot. Of course it sounds like somebody wants to come in the front door.

People will say, "One smile will get you a hundred." If you smile at somebody they'll smile back. I want you to try something. I want you to go into a situation with a complete stranger who is totally inert; they're not smiling, they're not grimacing. Just walk up to them, frown a little and say, "Smile, go on, smile."

No matter how bad you look, no matter how impassive you keep your face, what will happen is that if you repeat this with the intent and assurance of a hypnotist they will smile. That will work more than 90% of the time. If you're in a situation where you know for a fact that those people are somnambulists they won't be able to stop themselves. It will instantly happen!

And they will begin to feel happier emotionally! And that will be attached to you.

Remember that psychology and physiology are closely linked. The act of touching the side of my nose when I'm thinking about stuff is closely linked to what's going on in my head. If I want to get myself into the mood where I'm thinking about stuff I touch the side of my nose deliberately. It works in both directions, so when I start to smile, guess what? I go into a better mood.

Attachments work in both ways. These aren't anchors. These aren't things that keep people embedded somewhere that they're tugging at the anchor all the time, trying to move away from it. These aren't anchors. These are attachments. These are habits.

Remember, if you think it once it's a thought, if you think it seven times it's a habit. Repetition works!

Because you're attracting your core people now, you can just walk up to them and just say, "Smile," and they will. I do it a lot, especially with checkout operators. I know I write a lot about checkout operators the thing is you get to practice and unlike parties or networking meetings the outcome doesn't matter so the pressure is off.

Although I must put it on record that I haven't hypnotized any and got them to give me all the money out of the till, like that gentleman did in Italy last year, but you know, just getting people to smile is great! It gives you a buzz.

There's a lot of energy that passes between human beings. I'm not going to get too deeply into the energy thing because a lot of people don't like that, but at the end of the day that's all there is.

There isn't anything else. People talk about space and they say, "Oh, space is empty." No, it's not. It's full of energy. Energy is everywhere. We know for a fact that between ourselves we feel energy going from one to the other. So when we tell someone to smile, they start to smile, they start to feel good, that gives us a kick and makes us feel good, so everybody feels good. Great! Fabulous!

It's just as easy to make everybody feel bad. Just not as rewarding.

What I'm saying is keep it simple. You don't need to smile. The old phrase "if you're smiling everybody else around you will smile" isn't quite true because people aren't really looking at you. They're looking internally, especially if they're not smiling. If you tell them to smile they will. If you really demand it, if you repeat it, if you compound that, if you say, "Go on, smile, smile, go on, smile, you can't resist it, smile, smile, smile," you won't get past number seven. Try it. I promise you, it will work.

Now what have you done there? You actually created somebody who feels better when you're around!

How that works in a marketing term, how that works in a situation where you want to free up some time by getting people to do stuff for you, how that works is that *they're more likely to do you favours if they feel good when you're around.* End of story. It's very simple and easy.

What I'm doing in this course is to simplify what has become ridiculously complicated and complex. There are whole schools of thought now that if you don't go through all these complex and complicated routines that you can't do what you do.

As a hypnotist I do things very simply, very easily, and I get exactly the same results as people who take hours and hours to do it, days, and sometimes even twenty, thirty different meetings. In fact, more often than not, my results are better!

We just keep this simple. No, you don't have to smile; you just need to use the word. "Smile" is a hypnotic word because that smiling will bring forward dopamine; it will get them into a good mood. It will give them what they want as far as rewards are concerned.

# Installation

I'm going to tell you about the stuff I do, my favourite stuff: the way I install stuff in people when they come on courses, the way I install concepts in people. The world is caught up in the idea of building relationships. Certainly the marketing world is caught up more recently, where marketing, selling, getting people to work with you rather than against you all of that is now about building relationships.

Even the tough companies are more interested in building relationships. They're not very good at it! But at least they're more interested in building a relationship than they are in just getting customers, just getting clients, or just making money.

Even the clever pick-up artists, the clever people who are selling "how do I get that woman over there into bed" programs, are turning around and beginning to realize that there is more mileage and more reward about the people concerned when we go into a relationship rather than just going into a control or seduction thing.

The control thing is easy. It's simple. Get them into a state where they focus, and if you want to put them into a trance, grab hold of them anywhere, just grab hold of their elbow and just say, "Sleep!" and they'll go into a trance. If they are a somnambulist they won't be able to resist it!

If you're talking to somebody and you say, "Just look at that spot. Look at that spot there on the desk. Just look at it, look at it, look at it. Try and take your eyes away from it. Can you take your eyes away from it? You can't take your eyes away from it. Look at it, look at it, look at it. And just close your eyes and go into that deep hypnotic state." If you want to create that, that's easy. But DO NOT DO THIS YET make sure you read the Envoi at the end of the book!

Actually, if you do what I've just done, 20% of people will go into that hypnotic state. More than half will go into it with a little bit more effort. It's that simple. It's that easy. I've gone down from teaching hypnosis over five days to teaching it in a day because I've stripped out all the stuff that you actually don't need.

It's the same with this stuff. It's very simple. One of the hardest things I've got with students is telling them to turn their logic and their conscious off and start doing it simply.

People watch me. People watch me on the Internet. They watch me in classes and they watch me in social situations and they say, "How do you do it? How do you come across as being charismatic? How do you come across as being the centre of attention? How do you hold people like that? How do you actually do it?"

People who don't understand it can call it everything from charisma to arrogance and they can't understand that I'm not doing anything complex. They can't understand that I'm not doing anything that you can't actually see. All I'm doing is the simple stuff. All I'm doing is the stuff that is right out there.

I'm not really doing anything at all. I'm letting them do it.

# Awe Rapport

There's another rapport we can use.

I've talked about building up the relationship where you're on the same level as the person, where you're building friendship, where you're building rapport, which is empathy. That is, you're doing the same stuff, and you're heading towards the same goal. There's another rapport, another rapport we can use very simply, very easily.

I've said before that one of the most hypnotic words, *the* most hypnotic word you have got that beats the hell out of all other hypnotic words – and beats the crap out of any strange shit like pushing forward the sugar bowl or tapping teacups or anything like that – is to just use the word "hypnotist" or "hypnosis" if you want to get somebody in a hypnotic mood, just use that word.

Remember that my target market, my Core target, is a *Somnambulist*. There's no doubt about that. When I'm talking about Adam and when I'm talking about everything else, the one thing that goes at the top of the list is that Adam is a somnambulist. Adam is very easy to hypnotise. That's my target market.

How do I know that I'm going to get him? How do I know that he's going to be there? I tell him I'm a hypnotist with intent and if I don't get the right reaction I drop them and move on.

I know that thousands and thousands of people reading this book don't think they're hypnotists, but you can still use the word. You might say, "Oh, well, actually I'm a graphic designer and a hypnotist." Or you might say, "I'm an Internet marketer and a hypnotist." You might say, "I'm a singer and a hypnotist." As soon as you say *hypnotist* you can forget anything else that you tell them because if they are a somnambulist they will.

They will automatically be focused on the hypnotic state. As soon as you say the word hypnotist you're going to get one of two reactions. The first reaction you're going to get is fear. They're going to be scared. They're going to look at you and go, "Oh, God! Really?"

The second you get that, you've got an emotive state. You may think you haven't got a pleasant emotive state because the logical way to look at fear is of an unproductive, "bad" emotional state. That's wrong! Fear is a wonderful thing. It's a fantastic thing to experience!

Why do you think people jump out of airplanes at thirty thousand feet with a piece of silk tied to their back? Why do you think people go up and down on roller coaster rides at fairgrounds? Fear.

Why do you think people climb mountains, take risks? That rush of adrenaline. It's like a panic attack that they're actually enjoying!

Fear isn't a bad thing. If somebody says to me, "Oh, I'm scared of hypnosis," I'll say, "So you should be. We can do anything." Think about that. Fear really builds awe rapport.

That leads to the second thing that you want to get after telling someone that you're a hypnotist, which is, "Really? That's fascinating!" You're now in what I call, awe rapport. People are in awe of you. People think of hypnotists in exactly the same way they think of surgeons, in exactly the same way they think of top scientists, in exactly the same way they think of famous celebrities.

If you say Hypno*therapist*, of course, that's a totally different kettle of fish. People think of Hypno*therapists* the way they think of psychiatrists, psychologists. Psychiatrists and psychologists do not have awe rapport, not in the same way as you saying, "I'm a millionaire" or "I'm a brain surgeon."

\*\*\*\*\*\*\*\*\*\*\*\*\*\*\*\*\*\*\*\*\*\*\*\*\*\*\*\*\*\*\*\*\*\*\*\*\*\*\*\*\*\*\*\*\*\*

The word therapy immediately makes people think of being ill. Bad move even if you are a therapist to tell people. Unless you want to attract and influence the unwell of course.

\*\*\*\*\*\*\*\*\*\*\*\*\*\*\*\*\*\*\*\*\*\*\*\*\*\*\*\*\*\*\*\*\*\*\*\*\*\*\*\*\*\*\*\*\*\*

Awe rapport. Use it. It's a very valuable tool.

It's very easy to get somebody into awe rapport. Why do you use awe rapport? You use awe rapport to open up their subconscious mind so you can build a relationship. Don't ever think that you are doing anything else.

# Give Don't Sell

It's been called 'Moving the free line' in internet marketing. It used to be called doing demonstrations pre the world wide web. Basically it is a very old concept which works on the undeniable truth that the more you give the more you get.

How do we apply that to Influence?

Don't go into a situation thinking, "I'm going to sell you my services. I'm going to sell you my product."

Do think and intend, "I'm going to build a relationship with you. I'm going to advise you and give you all the stuff you need and sooner or later you're going to turn around and ask me to sell you something."

This is the New Age for marketing. This is what Tim Ferris talks about in his book, *The Four Hour Work Week* when he mentions the new rich. It's what Internet Marketers like my friend Alex Mandossian, Frank Kerns are saying. It's what leaders in the Persuasion and Influence field are saying, people like Dave Lakhani and Kevin Hogan. It's a way of shifting perspective. Instead of selling to people we give to people, and then they ask to buy. Very often they'll ask to buy the very thing you gave them.

It's scary at first. Believe me, Jane and I have been going through this with our Academy of Hypnotic Arts and other online business recently and it is scary at first. But, you know, as I was writing this book we put out an email letter announcing the next hypnosis training. Within the first few minutes, two people went and bought courses and one guy said, "I can't make it! When are you doing the next one? Sell me something!" We build relationships with people.

All this covert core stuff isn't about controlling. It's about building relationships.

Does that mean you can't control? No, I've told you how to do that. Very simply, very easily you can put people into hypnotic states. If they're a somnambulist they'll go into a hypnotic state. If they're not a somnambulist you'll never get them into a hypnotic state even if you're doing it up front with the world's biggest swinging watch. You'd have to hit them across the back of the head with a hammer to get something that even looks like trance.

Certainly using the awe rapport and hypnotic words and parroting will get them toward a hypnotic state. You can hypnotize them, then tell them they're going to do this, this, and this and they're going to forget about you afterwards. Great. Sounds fantastic. But sooner or later they're going to realize that something happened.

There's a story that a mentor of mine used to tell me how he went into a bank at the time when bank managers actually made the decisions about loans. I don't know about the rest of the world, but certainly in Britain that doesn't happen anymore. All a bank manager does is put your data out into the computer and a computer makes the decision about the loan, so please don't think you're going to use this to get the bank manager to give you a loan with little or no interest.

At the time when my mentor was doing this it was a case that the bank manager not only decided on whether you got the loan or not but also what interest would be charged. The situation was that when he went into the bank manager's office, the bank manager says, "What do you do for a living?" He said, "Well, I'm an entertainer and I do some magic, I do some mentalism, I throw some knives, and I'm a hypnotist."

"Oh, really? Oh, you're a hypnotist? Oh, very good, very good. I've seen a hypnotist on stage, but one mustn't get up, you know, because of one's position."

So my Mentor asked, "Do your hands stick together at the shows?"

He said, "Oh yes. Always."

Casually the Hypnotist said, "Like your hands are stuck to the desk?"

The manager tries to lift his hands from the desk. "Oh, God! That's very good, that's *very* good!"

My mentor walked out of that office with a mortgage with a very, *very* low interest. Fortunately, he doesn't even live in this country anymore so you can't get him! The point is, though, that he walked out with a very, very low interest.

The problem was a few months later he got a letter from the bank wanting to know why he got such a low interest.

People aren't islands. If you want to get somebody to buy your something and they buy it and they take it home, they're going to show it to people that you haven't influenced and hypnotized. Never sell anybody something that can come back at you.

Build a relationship so that when they come back into your life it's in a good way. If you're coming from a place where Ethics go out the window then you will get caught.

Awe rapport. Can we use that? We use awe rapport to open the door. We use our position to open the door.

# The Confidence Trick

That leads me to the next thing, the thing that I call "the confidence trick." When I say *confidence trick,* most people would think of going into a situation where you get somebody's confidence, you get them to know, like, and trust you and then you sell them something, or you sell them an idea, or you get them to do something that's detrimental to them, they give you their life's saving, you give them nothing and you walk away from it. You've got lots of money and you don't care about that person, blah, blah, blah, blah, blah.

That's not what I mean when *I* talk about the confidence trick. I'm talking about the trick of being confident – so confident in what you do, it just cannot *not* work. We get back to the very beginning – we get back to intent.

Your confidence is a trick you can use over and over and over again. If you're in a situation where the other person's confidence in you seems to be waning somewhat, it's very easy and simple to shift the conversation to something you are confident about.

There's something in your life right now that you can talk about forever and that you're extremely confident about. It doesn't have to be the thing that you're there for, because conversations with friends don't work like that. Conversations with friends go all over the place. People accept that.

Remember that you're talking to a friend. When you remember that you're talking to a friend (and you're talking to a nine-year-old friend), you can take the conversation wherever you like.

They will allow you to shoot off at a tangent and will think that something they said inspired you to think of this thing you are obviously passionate and enthusiastic about. Remember just as no one accepts blame; no one is prepared to think that they are not entirely influential either. Not a bad thing as influence is a two way street.

When you do change the conversation to take it wherever you like, you're doing what the NLP'ers calls a pattern interrupt! You're confusing the conscious mind and then you start talking directly to the subconscious.

I just talk directly to the subconscious all the time, which usually confuses the conscious mind in 99.9% of the cases.

The confidence trick is simply being confident. The trick is to talk about something that you are confident about at the time when you need the extra confidence.

The easiest way of doing that is to drop into telling a story. Don't make the story something with a moral or make a story up or anything like that. Regardless of whatever the conversation you've been having has dropped you into, start thinking about something that you're confident in, something that you absolutely know for sure, then drop into that. Something you have really done, an absolute truth of yours. Talk about it for a few seconds and then come out.

What happens then is psychological and physiological. You sit up straighter, you're more confident, you're happier, and when you're confident and happy you know that they're in rapport with you. You don't need to do anything special. You just have to look back to your core and make your core come out.

The Confidence Trick. It's simple, easy, and anybody can do it at any time.

I've taught this to actors, I've taught it to people going on stage. I've certainly taught it to people in most of my stage hypnosis courses. People don't mind you rambling and you can be confident they're happy with you being confident. They want their expert to be confident!

# The Give Me More Pattern

Very often all this leads to what I call the "give me more" pattern. The give me more pattern. We are greedy beasts. We are totally, completely, and absolutely greedy. When we get something we like, when we experience something that's awesome, we want more.

It's not just the case of opening the box and eating one donut when there's another one there, and another and another. Human beings like excess.

If you're feeding someone that feel-good factor, they will come back time and time and time again for more. I was once part of a group where we were talking about the ethics of using anchors, using attachments. One of the participants, an American Hypnotist friend of mine called Jeff Stephens talked about getting a waitress in a restaurant to feel good when she was serving him so he got better service. She had a more enjoyable evening because of it.

One thing that I remember him saying was that every time she came past his table, he did something specific and she smiled. I think it was something like tapping the table with a pen and she smiled.

As an interested observer, I would have loved to have counted the number of times she came past his table compared to everybody else's because it would have increased.

It would have increased because people want more and will come back for more. You deliver the goods and they'll come back for more. We've got people on our marketing list now who write to us

213

all the time asking. "What else are you doing? I've got this, I've got this, I've bought that, I've got everything you've done. When are you going to do something else? When can I come back for more?"

\* \* \* \* \* \* \* \* \* \* \* \* \* \* \* \* \* \* \* \* \* \* \* \* \* \* \* \* \* \* \* \* \* \* \* \* \* \* \* \* \* \* \* \* \* \* \* \*

Talking to Jeff later he told me she even detoured across the room to pass close by.

\* \* \* \* \* \* \* \* \* \* \* \* \* \* \* \* \* \* \* \* \* \* \* \* \* \* \* \* \* \* \* \* \* \* \* \* \* \* \* \* \* \* \* \* \* \* \* \*

The "give me more" pattern is embedded in every single human being. It's how we survive.

You don't have to create that – you just have to fire it. Remember, you don't create this stuff, you're **using** it. There's nothing fancy to create. You're just using it, and you're going to use it all the time. The more you use it the less you'll remember that you used it. You're going to get to the point when in a month or two month's time you'll really have to think, "How did that work? How did that happen? How did I get that deal?" Because you'll be doing it *automatically*.

The only reason that I'm actually now pulling these things out and thinking about things like, "How did I get that person to do that? How did I, didn't I? What did I say? What did I do?" is because I'm teaching it, and as you teach something you look at it in an entirely different way.

Again, as you teach something you look at it in an entirely different way. By the time you have been using these skills for a month or more, unless you're teaching somebody else to use them, you won't even remember using them. You'll just know that life's changed because it will all be automatic. It will be installed.

What do you do with the "give me more" pattern? You do exactly that! The more they come back for more, the more you give. The more they ask, the more you give. You're still not selling anybody anything. You're still giving to them.

Eventually they'll come back and say, "Let me pay for this." "Let me do something for you."

Take that metaphorically too, because that goes for every situation in your life. Eventually they'll say, "Look, you've given me all this good stuff, you've done something wonderful for me. Let me do something wonderful for you." That's the payoff time. That's where you get the "what's in it for me." What's in it for you is the payback time.

Different people will give to you in different ways at different times, but you will get it all back and more. And don't think that they're thinking, "What's in it for me?" all the time because the more you give you go beyond the "What's in it for me" into, "What's in it for you? What can I give you? Have I said thank you? How do I give you your reward? "

Remember the five steps to using influence:

**Intent:** knowing exactly what it is you want to achieve, remove doubt and, focus on the result.

**Observe:** watch and listen for their trance moments, their subconscious words, their attachments. Use them – don't use your own. Why create a situation where you're teaching them something? Just use what they've already got on board.

**Rapport:** parrot build rapport. Use awe rapport. Don't mirror stuff – match it exactly.

**Access the mind:** fire imagination and emotion, trigger pattern changes by suggesting them directly.

**Test:** test the result. Attempt to trigger the old pattern.

If you get somebody in a good mood it's very easy to test if they're in a good mood: you say, "Are you happy now?"

"Yeah, yeah."

The big test is if you can trigger the old pattern. Can you trigger the miserable person that you met at the start of the day? Can you get them to do what they used to do before? If the reason you're doing this is to stop them doing something, try triggering that pattern. If they can override what you put in, if they can override the smile and go back to feeling miserable again then you haven't put the pattern in strong enough.

I really want to make that point. Testing isn't about "Will they do what I've told them to?" It's actually about "Will they do the old stuff and override what I've told them to?" They shouldn't be able to do that.

# The Emotional Tools of Influence

There are five things that drive us and because it's the natural drives you are using to influence there are therefore five emotional tools of influence.

**Compliance**: compliance is the desire to be the same, socially accepted by our peers. It's one of our biggest drives. One of your biggest drives is to be in with the in crowd, to comply with society, to be part of the gang. That's exactly how gangs work. It's how tribes work. It's how groups of business people work. Sometimes it's even how families work, although nowadays that's not as true is it? Actually it's even more like that now.

The desire to be the same, to be socially accepted by peers, is a very strong driving force in our society. It's an emotional tool that you can use. They want to be the same.

Think Clubs, Gangs, Cults...

**Achievement**: the desire to win, the desire to feel that you have achieved something, the desire to feel that you've got somewhere, you've achieved your goal, you've become successful. How can you use achievement? Just make them feel that they've won!

**Recognition:** the desire to be known. This is certainly a driver of mine! I have the desire to be known throughout the world as the world's greatest teacher of this stuff. I think I already am, and lots of other people do (and by making a joke of it by the way, I'm deeply embedding that into your subconscious mind, but don't worry. Don't worry about that because your subconscious mind won't notice, and your conscious mind can't stop me).

**Importance**: importance is actually the desire to be of value, to be significant, to feel important.

When I was nursing I worked with a lot of paraplegics and quadriplegics with spinal injuries. When I had really helped somebody achieve something, learn something new, some way of getting out of the wheelchair on their own or something like that, I went home with a deep feeling of fulfilment and satisfaction. I had a deep feeling of importance and significance. I had been significant in somebody's life.

I get that a lot in what I do now. I feel of value and significance toward people – and I am because I'm so good at what I do!

**Reward**: the desire to receive what one deserves. The desire to get people to say to me, "That was so good. Here's this." Getting their token of appreciation, which in our society is usually money, and because I'm so good I get to see quite a bit of that, which is great! That's fabulous, and I'm really, really grateful for it.

And even though I'm doing this "I'm so good at what I do I can implant it into your mind" thing, and I'm doing it so blatantly, so openly, and you're even beginning to notice it now because I'm pushing it even further in front than I did before, it doesn't matter, because it's still working. It's still going into your head. And it's going into your head, and it's going into your subconscious mind, and it's going into your special place, and it's going into your receptacle, and it's becoming a part of you. And when you think of me, you fire those attachments, you fire those emotions. You have no choice!

You just don't have any choice. You have no choice. Repetition works so incredibly well!

# Putting it All Together

How do we put all this together?

Use the Five steps:

- **Intent**

- **Observe**

- **Rapport**

- **Access the mind = suggest.**

- **Test**

Before you go out, you know what you're going to do. When you're there, you watch. After watching, you decide who you are going to do it with, you bring them in, and you make friends. You get a relationship going.

Then you create a situation once you've got them into the relationship with you, once you've got them into hypnosis, once you've got them into that connection where they're responding to the things that you're giving them and the concepts that you're giving them and they're feeling really good (believe me you want their head full of dopamine because a head full of dopamine remembers better, retains more, and learns more), then you access their mind, you fire their imagination and emotion, you trigger pattern changes by suggesting to them directly.

Use those important words like *you, want, have, will, do, must, always.*

By suggesting directly I mean saying, "Oh, you always do that."

If they say, "No I don't," respond with, "Yes…"

Or say, "You want this."

They ask, "Want what?"

"This. Look."

If you get caught, don't back off. You're playing a game!

And then you test. You test the result. You must test, because if you don't test, you don't know. If you don't test, you don't know.

That way, you're firing the emotional tools of influence, the compliance, achievement, recognition, importance, and the reward. When talking directly to the subconscious mind simple phrasing works best. It's the conscious mind that's looking for complexity. This is the beautiful thing about the conscious mind: the conscious mind is looking for complexity, therefore when you give it simplicity, it will ignore it as being inconsequential and unimportant! Think about that.

Think about all the times your conscious mind has just thrown something away because it didn't look important or complicated enough. You just ignored it consciously and still reacted to it subconsciously. As any magician will tell you, the simplest way of misdirecting the eye is to point in the opposite direction of where you want them to look. Their eyes will go where you point. Big deal! It's an attachment. It's a habit.

It's not an anchor. Remember, anchors keep you where you are. Attachments move with you. Patterns move with you. Habits move with you. You point, they look. In that second, you're doing something in the opposite direction. This is exactly the same.

The covert conversational stuff is exactly the same. You don't have to hide it in complex, complicated algorithms of language. Put it straight out in front. If it's so simple, and it's way blatant, the conscious mind will go, "Ha ha ha, it can't be that simple," and it will ignore it. When the conscious mind ignores it, the subconscious mind takes notice.

The language pattern stuff works ok. But it works despite of the awkward and lengthy approaches. Mainly because it serves to focus the intent of the hypnotist rather than because it's all powerful. The truth is this stuff works better, faster, simpler, easier, and there's nothing to remember! But remember you will.

Put it all together with those five little, simple steps that you're taking. I'm not saying that there's not more stuff, that there are not questions you could ask, and I'm not saying that the NLP stuff is not very good – a lot of it is when it comes down to accessing different levels of consciousness. I'm just saying that you should remember that we're not dealing with the conscious mind at all.

We're not dealing with the conscious brain at all. We're dealing with the subconscious mind – a bright child. And that's how I'm implanting it in you.

This time I'm implanting it in you so strongly because I'm repeating it over and over and over again, and you have probably noticed it now, but it doesn't matter, because I'm not interested in whether or not your conscious mind/brain has noticed it or not! And yeah, I'm a cocky bastard because I'm really, really good at what I do.

So what am I installing?

First you get your intent. What's your intent? What's in it for you? What do you want out of the thing? You're going into a situation and this is going to be turned on. It's not a process that you turn on, where you go into a situation and think that you're going to do all of this to get these results, and for the rest of the day you're going to be totally inert and do nothing. Once this is in, it's who you are, not what you do.

I say this time and time again: life isn't a problem to be sorted. It's an experience to be enhanced! It goes on forever. This stuff is continuous. It goes on. It's not just a case of going into a situation to see if you can stick somebody to a wall. That's easy. That's no problem.

When people ask me what I do, I say I'm a hypnotist. My epiphany was that for a while I got away from that, trying to be a motivationalist, and then trying to be this, that, and the other. Lots of people who know me, though, have said that since I did my Core Rapport

I have become totally focused again, and that I've come back to being the Hypnotist! It's not what I do. It's *who I am*!

Your mind will figure out how to put it all together anyway, and what to do next. And then it becomes a pattern. And when it becomes a pattern you repeat it, and when you repeat it, it becomes a habit. When it becomes a habit you stop thinking about it.

Oh good Lord, I haven't done a stage show now since August of 2008, but if you put me in front of two thousand people in a theatre, I would give a show like you wouldn't believe. I don't even have to think about it. It isn't something I have to turn on; it's just something I do. It's like putting my pants on in the morning. I don't think about it.

You're going to get to the point – and you are at that point – where once you have done this two, four, five, seven times, you stop thinking about. You just do it all the time. All the time! It becomes the game you play all the time. It becomes the ultimate boys toy.

It's not a case of how much you can get out of a person. It's a case of just accepting that it's just coming to you all the time. It's an experiment: "Let's see what will happen when I press this button. Wow!"

And that will happen to you even as you're reading this book, because what you're going to do is you're going to find that you want to read this more than once, and you'll be reading it and reading it and reading it, because repetition puts it into your head.

The beautiful thing about repetition as well is that when you say something to somebody once, they might hear it. When you say something to them twice, they might notice. When you say it to them three times, it's part of your speech pattern. As far as their conscious mind is concerned, it turns off. They stop hearing that phrase anymore.

By the time you've done it seven times, your conscious mind won't even notice that you're doing it anymore. You will have learned it!

And it doesn't matter whether you want to use this to sell a hypnosis show to somebody, whether you want to use it to sell hypnosis sessions, whether you want to use this to sell stocks and shares, whether you want to use this to sell dog training, whether you want to use this to sell the fact that you might be the person that they might want to spend the rest of their lives with, or whether you want to sell them the idea that being around you is really good and they ought to want that more. It really doesn't matter!

Basically, to the subconscious mind, there is no difference. Stuff just makes you feel good, and the subconscious mind doesn't think in the way that your conscious mind does, with ideas like "That's expensive; that's not." It doesn't even come into it. That's conscious, logical shit. Your subconscious mind doesn't give a shit about that because it doesn't care about it.

Because it's not pointed at that and nothing else, it starts to play, and as soon as it starts to play, you become charismatic, as soon as you become charismatic, people give you stuff! It gets to the point where Elton John could make the world's worst album next year and it will sell out.

It's not a case of where you get that from. It's a case of realizing that it's out there, that people want to give it to you! Just like when you give someone a smile and make them feel good, and that makes you feel good, people want to give you stuff because they want to feel good as well. It's a natural human drive.

It's not what you do. Don't think of this as something you do. It becomes part of who you are. You get to that point where it stops being a conscious thought, where because of the repetition it stops being a conscious thought, and it starts becoming part of your subconscious process. When it becomes part of your subconscious process you'll go, "Wow! I don't need to learn this anymore!"

It's just like that moment that most people forget, but that wonderful moment of achievement when you rode the bike for the first time and you didn't fall over. Then you start to enjoy all this stuff, and once you start to enjoy it your life gets *massive*. When you're doing what you are born do to – and you were born to do this – you can't think of anything else!

I don't want you to have short-term rapport. Short-term rapport and short-term reward are a waste of time. It's a waste of your life. I know because I've been there and done that. Sometimes even when you're using these techniques with people that you know very well, it still sometimes takes some time, but it's only a case of waiting for the right time to happen.

# CLASS 5

## ACTION SECTION

Intent - Observe - Rapport
Access their mind - Test

# How do you make it work?
## Test

This class deals with testing your results to attempt to trigger the old patterns.

These are the steps that we have taken you through so far:

1. **Intent** - Know what you want to achieve

2. **Observe** - Listen and observe the person's subconscious

3. **Rapport** - Parrot the other person exactly

4. **Access their mind** - Fire the person's imagination and emotions

**5. Test**
The final step, testing, is important because if you don't test your results, you won't know for sure whether or not you have got results.

So how do you test your work?

You attempt to trigger the old pattern to see if it has changed.

Repetition is extremely important

When you say something to someone once or twice they might hear it. But when you say it three times, it becomes part of someone's subconscious. They have learned it.

We learn by seeing words associated with things over and over. This is how the subconscious mind works.

We call this compounding a suggestion. Compound it in until it sticks.

The key to compounding a suggestion is to do the following:

- **Important Words**

- **Repetition**

## Emotional Tools of Influence

There are five steps of influence that are important to recognise. In order for stuff to work the following steps must be present:

1. Compliance

2. Achievement

3. Recognition

4. Importance

5. Reward

scared to repeat things when they are doing
. We don't want to get discovered.

ve are *playing a game and experimenting*.
vered? After all, when you explain what you
respond positively!

Émile Coué invented,

way, I am getting better and better."

imes a day in the morning and in the night.
I see this to be true.

and see how you feel after saying this phrase 7
- 10 times.

## The Reason This Process Works is…

If you think something repetitively (at least 7 times), it will always
work.

## Anchoring and Attachments:

The term "anchoring" is a part of NLP. Certain anchors bring forth
certain effects. An attachment or a habit is a much better way of
thinking of anchoring.

When you are influencing someone, always use simple and predictable attachments, preferably his or her own!

---

Important step

Ask someone their name and repeat it several times in a sentence. This is a very powerful tool in creating influence.

---

## Start to Observe Patterns:

When you observe someone, you will notice they have patterns (which is perhaps an easier way of thinking of anchors and attachments). Maybe when they are sad, they will touch the back of their neck. Maybe they look up. Watch and take notice of what people's patterns are. You are dealing with the subconscious mind.

## Try this Easy Exercise:

1.    Hit an emotion that you want to produce in that person

2.    Watch what they do in response.

Now that you know their patterns, you are freed up to mirror these patterns. When you want to fire a certain emotion, do what they are doing. Watch their emotions.

Experiment with this process and watch the results!

By the way, no one will notice you are doing this mirroring. This is something insignificant. They don't notice they are doing it subconsciously, so they won't notice you do it.

## Exercise: Get Someone into a Good Mood

When you want to get someone into a good mood, you want to build concepts into their head.

*Here is one way you can do it:*

1.  Walk up to a complete stranger (Obviously do this in a social or business situation where this won't get you a sexual harassment charge or result in your face getting turned inside out.)

2.  Frown a little

3.  Tell the person to smile. Keep compounding - repeating - that one word until you get the smile.

You will find this exercise works succesfully more than 80% of the time! Psychology and physiology are closely interlinked. When someone starts to smile, he or she gets into a better mood.

Another way you can get someone into a good mood is as follows:

1.  Notice someone in an annoyed or "bad" mood.

2.  Say to them directly, "Don't be in a bad mood."

Remember, we are talking to a bright 9 year old child. When you strip everything down, we all want to play.

## More Tricks You Can Use

1.   Say you are a hypnotist

Saying you are a hypnotist is extremely powerful. You can even just say that you dabble in hypnosis or know some hypnosis. Once you have told someone you are a hypnotist, one of two things will happen.

a.   The first thing is you will get the immediate reaction of fear. (However, don't worry, you aren't doing something negative. People often enjoy the emotion of fear. Why else would they go on roller coasters, sky dive, etc?)

b.   The second possible reaction is awe. The person will light up and say that is really fascinating. This creates Awe Rapport.

### *How can we use Awe Rapport?*

Awe rapport can open the door to being very influential! This is also a tool you should keep in mind. Use this tool when you can.

2.   Use Awe Rapport

Once you have someone in awe rapport, you can sooner or later get him or her to buy something or do whatever you want him or her to do.

Awe rapport opens up people's subconscious mind. They are then in a good situation to receive your influence.

3.  Give People Something of Value

Instead of going out of our way to sell someone something, we are giving information and building relationships.

This process isn't about controlling. It strictly focuses on making these relationships and giving people something of value.

When you give someone something of value, the person automatically thinks, "You have done something wonderful for me, let me do something wonderful for you."

Then before you know it is "payback time." You will then get something back. At this point, you will find that they ASK how to buy.

The more you give, they will want to say thank you. They will say, "how do I give you your reward?"

4.  Confidence Streak

Another trick you can use is to be so confident that whatever you are doing will indeed work. This point gets back to our first lesson on Intent.

Your confidence is a trick that you can use over and over again.

*How do we effectively use confidence?*

If you are in a situation where your confidence is waning, shift the conversation to something you are 100% confident about.

Here is why this will work

—People don't mind you rambling.

—When you are confident, it will make people happy.

—Confidence can lead to the "give me more" pattern. People are greedy and will then want more of your confidence.

This "give me more" pattern is embedded in every person. You just have to excite, access and use this pattern. It is already installed in people.

## Summary

When you have people in the moment when they are responding to what you are doing (with their heads full of dopamine), they remember better and respond more.

This works so well because you are communicating with their bright 9-year-old child.

Trigger pattern changes by suggesting these changes directly.

# ENVOI

The Wake Up!

## Envoi:

There are people in the world for who being hypnotised, being in an accepting state for suggestion, is not a choice. Not ever, never.

Those people will with very little effort, certainly less than the effort you will be applying to this, enter the state that everyone over the age of five in the western world would recognize as hypnosis. That is full blown trance hypnosis.

When this happens you will know because it's characterized by either a stare or closed eyes, apparent lack of attention to any exterior stimulus, absolute acceptance and performance of every suggestion the person who is their hypnotist gives them. And the worst if you are not expecting it, huge emotional reaction and demonstration such as crying, screaming, laughing, hysteria. Extremely rare even in formal hypnosis but so are car accidents however we still put on our safety belts do we not?

If this happens you need to know what to do.

DON'T PANIC!

**If they are somnambulistic, and it's only these who will react large, tell them to stop. Then terminate the session.**

# THE WAKE UP SCRIPT

You:

**One!**

Every nerve, every muscle becoming less relaxed.

**Two:**

Feel that huge surge of energy go right through your body.

**Three:**

Take a deep, deep breath of cool clear mountain air, feeling that energy giving oxygen going through every nerve muscle and fibre.

**Four:**

you can feel that cool clear mountain water washing through your head, your chest, your body. Your stomach and chest are clear. Your head is clear. Your throat and nose are clear. Your eyes are bright and shiny and -

**Five!** WIDE AWAKE!"

Make every word a direct command. Lift your voice as you go through the numbers and emphasise the emotive words and action words such as 'clear', 'energy' and 'bright and shiny'

## Svengali System - Online Installation Classes

**You've read the book**

**NOW**

Really put these techniques to use by having Jonathan Chase install the concepts and principles of the Svengali System directly into you.

21 Audios, 5 Action Workbooks, a 200+ page EBook copy of the accompanying book, 21 downloadable MP3 files for iTunes, iPhone, Blackberry or your favourite MP3 player.

In the old days that would have been put in a nice Big Box and it would have a similar carbon footprint of a medium sized SUV four wheeled drive jeep.

It would take three weeks to print, wrap and pack and anywhere from 3 days to three months to deliver.

Now, thanks to the gloriously almost instant technology afforded by the InterWeb we can deliver said package to You in moments - or at the very worst in a couple of hours - so that You Can Get The Best from this Life Enhancing Training where, when and how You choose.

Go and sign up now JonathanChase.com

## Other Titles by Jonathan Chase
### *from the Academy of Hypnotic Arts*

"I don't suffer from what I call 'The Bigger the Book – the Better the System' Syndrome, a condition where the heaviness of the book is more important than the weight of the content, so I write what works in a format you can slip in a purse or pocket without losing too much cash from either, the rest is already out there if you've got a wheelbarrow."
Jonathan Chase

**Deeper and Deeper** – *the secrets of stage hypnosis*

Jonathan Chase's first published book is considered by many to be The Reference for the entertainment section of the art.

**Don't Look In His Eyes!** – *how to be a confident original hypnotist*

In Don't Look In His Eyes, Jonathan shares his encyclopedic knowledge and experience of consulting hypnosis that has forged his maverick reputation, keeping it simple and sincere.

**Other titles available from JonathanChase.com**

# GET MORE FROM SVENGALI ALLIANCE

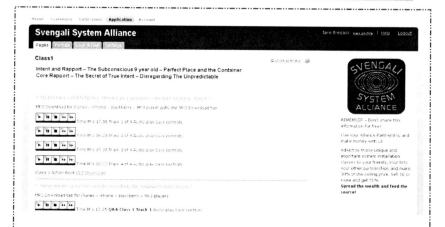

## Online InterWeb Training

The full live recorded audio class this book is based on is available for download now from the internet at JonathanChase.com

**Earn Money with us** - We run an affiliate system where you can earn cash just by telling your friends about the Svengali System

**Learn about** our Weekend Seminars and Full Week Intensive Mind Changing **MORE Experiences** including the Svengali System and Jon Chase's Success Cycle.

**Learn Hypnosis** - not just the covert stuff but the full blown watch swinging mind control hypnosis.

**Listen** to Jon's The Hypnotist Radio show and read his Blog.

## Just come to JonathanChase.com and get MORE

Lightning Source UK Ltd.
Milton Keynes UK
UKOW021407051211

183232UK00011B/89/P